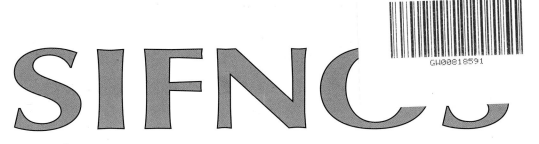

SIFNOS

the light of Apollo

EDITIONS
TOUBI'S®
ΕΚΔΟΣΕΙΣ

Texts: ANNA MARANTI (Archaeologist)
Text editing: DAPHNE CHRISTOU
Natural environment: YIORGOS SFIKAS
Geological details: VASSILIS TSELEPIDIS
Translation: JUDY GIANNAKOPOULOU
Artistic Supervision: EVI DAMIRI
Photographs: DORA KOLIOPANOU, KOSTAS KOUNADIS, ARCHIVES M. TOUBIS S.A.

Colour separations and printing: M. TOUBIS GRAPHIC ARTS S.A.

We would like to express our warmest thanks for their advice during the writing of this book to Mr and Mrs Kounadi.

Copyright © 2002 MICHALIS TOUBIS EDITIONS S.A., Tel.: (010) 6029974, Fax: 6646856 – Athens
INTERNET: http://www.toubis.gr
ISBN: 960-540-370-6

5 - 2005

Example of a parish* church in Sifnos.

* The churches in Sifnos which have a blue dome are called parish churches.
These churches are the only ones which are in use.

*To whatever of its corners I may wander,
all I need is the misty pink of eventide
that I may find my soul wandering
along the stone-paved of Sifnos.*

*Snow white walls, domes of azure,
fragrance of jasmine and nightblooming flowers
sail the Aegean together.*

*So small an island
yet touched by the infinite.*

ELLI KANELLOU-KOUNADI

CONTENTS

1   SIFNOS

Mountainous Sifnos makes its own distinctive contribution to the beauty of the Cycladic landscape. The hills and valleys verdant with olive trees make this Aegean island very much different from the others, with their minimal vegetation. The beauties of this island are not visible at first glance. When travellers coming to the island by ship hear the announcement that the boat is about to dock, they will see the slopes of two steep hills in the distance and will just be able to make out the houses of a town. This is Kamares, which will certainly delight the visitor, imprinting itself forever on the memory of the most

demanding traveller. But discovering Sifnos, the island of Apollo, takes time. It is not generous with its charms. It will reveal its hidden beauty a little at a time but will amply reward whoever has the inclination and the patience to get to know it better. From this viewpoint Sifnos is not the place for people looking for a programmed type of holiday. On the contrary, it is for travellers who take into account more than just the first impression of a place. Such people will appreciate the radiant light of Sifnos.

View of the town and island of Sifnos. Copper plate print, J.B. Hilaer, engraved by P.F. Hoffard, Gennadio Library, Athens.

The port of Kamares (view from Ayios Symeon).

Here, for a start, you can see Cycladic architecture in all its glory, in forms that are simple and absolutely in harmony with the needs and aesthetic character of the location. Dazzling white cube-shaped village houses, flagstone lanes whitewashed at the edges of the stones. Insinuating themselves in between are the perfumes and colours of lovely spring flowers. Friendly courtyards with white stone benches, and here and there picturesque churches with blue or white domes and elaborate belltowers.

Sifnos is waiting for us to stroll through its lanes, to enjoy the sunshine, to swim off its unspoilt beaches, to say a prayer at the church of the Panayia Ouranofora. And when the day shows the first signs of flagging, an equally enticing night awaits to lure us into other byways.

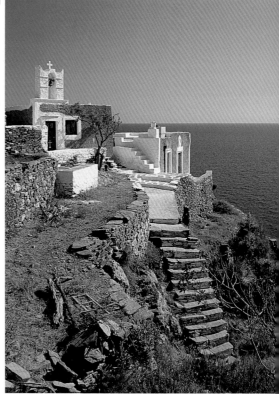

1. *The Church of the Saviour on the road towards Panayia Poulati.*
2. *Panayia Poulati.*
3. *The beach at Apokofto.*

Geography

Sifnos is one of the group of Aegean islands known as the Western Cyclades, and is situated at latitude 37 degrees 1 minute and longitude 24 degrees 43 minutes, in the centre of a triangle defined by the islands of Serifos, Kimolos and Antiparos. Triangular in shape, the island is 75 nautical miles from the port of Piraeus. It is 74 square kilometres in area. Its coastline, punctuated by numerous picturesque coves and inlets, is approximately 70 km in length. According to the latest population census (1991) Sifnos has 1958 permanent residents.

Administratively Sifnos belongs to the prefecture of the Cyclades, with its capital at Ermoupolis, Syros. It is under the ecclesiastical authority of the diocese of Syros. Recently it became an independent municipality following the amalgamation of the two local councils of Apollonia and Artemonas, and now includes - apart from those two villages - the settlements of Katavati, Exambela, Kato Petali, Ano Petali, Kastro, Faros, Platis Yialos, Vathi, Chrysopiyi, Kamares, Ayios Loukas, Troullaki and Herronissos. The seat of the new municipality is at Apollonia.

Morphology

The island is mountainous, with hills and small fertile valleys, densely planted with olive trees. Its highest point, the peak of the Profitis Ilias, is to be found in the central part of the island and is 680 metres above sea level. It is followed by Ayios Symeon, Profitis Ilias Troullakiou and Ayios Andreas, at altitudes of 490 m., 465 m. and 425 m. respectively. The Leivadas stream, 5.5 km in length, springs up in the central part of the island and flows into Kamares bay. There is also another 3-kilometre-long stream crossing the island. This is Erkeies which appears in the eastern part of Sifnos and flows into the cove of Seralia Kastrou. Characteristic features of the Sifnos geomorphology are the scenic sun-drenched inlets and bays that make up its coastline. Its small headlands are adorned with pretty chapels and look like something out of a picture gallery, as they stand framed against the vast blue of the Aegean. The modern visitor can enjoy the sandy beaches of Herronissos in the north, those of Vathi, Platis Yialos, Faros and Apokoftos in the south, of Kamares in the west and of Seralia in the east with its sparkling pebble beaches.

There are no other smaller islands around Sifnos, apart from the bare uninhabited islet of Kitriani to the south, near the promontory of Kontos.

Climate

Travellers visiting Sifnos in the last few centuries have made frequent mention of its exceptional climate. Summer is marvellous, with one sunny day after another, while winter is mild, with infrequent - but heavy - rain and extremely rare frosts and snowfall. There are prevailing strong winds from the north and the famous meltemia winds, chiefly in summertime.

Geology

Geotectonically, the island of Sifnos belongs to the Attic-Cycladic zone and consists almost exclusively of crystalline schists of various types containing rocks and minerals such as amphibole, hornblende, epidote, and micaceous gneiss, as well as marble, glauconite, phyllite, quartzite, etc. Of secondary importance and over a limited area, Pleistocene formations can be found with breccia and conglomerate rock, and finally Holocene formations with sand, shingles, and sediments deposited by streams in the regions of Kamares, Vathi and Platis Yialos. The island's metamorphic rock belongs to the underlying Attic-Cycladic crystalline schists. The entire system of crystalline rock has folded. The main fold runs in a NW-SE direction. Gneiss, schists and amphibolites occupy the entire southeastern part of the island as well as isolated sections in the south. The remainder (west and north) are occupied by dolomitised marble intrusions of gneiss from microcrystal to macrocrystal forms. In the northwest part of the island one also encounters gneiss, schist, glauconite and quartzite.

Ores of iron and manganese can be found today chiefly on the sites of Ayios Sostis (10 m. altitude), Ayios Sylvestros (300 m), Voreini (260 m.) Kapsalo and Polonia (310 m.) Tsigoura (320 m.), Xero Xylo (510 m.), Faros (70 m.), Skafi (290 m.), Klimati (250 m.).

Ferromanganese minerals are found within the marble horizon in lenticular forms, intrusions, etc. Sifnos has been known for its minerals since antiquity. They are reported in Pausanias, Herodotus, Strabo and Pliny. Legend says that Sifnos used to be rich in iron, lead, gold and silver, but that from the time the Sifnians once disregarded Apollo's command to send their tribute to Delphi in the form of a gold egg, and sent a gold-plated egg instead of a solid gold one, the sea inundated and destroyed the mines. The best known mines in antiquity were two: on the site of present-day Ayios Sostis, and at Kapsalo or Schismadi. In the former, which was flooded by the sea when the land subsided, there were many galleries and other installations. The Tsigoura mine has been known for 800 years and that of Voreini for 500 years.

Natural environment

In prehistoric times Sifnos, like all Cycladic islands, was uninhabited, covered with forests and rich in animal life. This situation began to change in the Neolithic period, during which man arrived and started burning the forests in order to clear the land for fields and pastures. Thus the Cycladic landscape as we know it today slowly came into being. Its predominant elements were scrub in places where the terrain was utilised as grazing land, and terracing wherever cereals, vines, or less frequently olives were cultivated.

There were times when systematic cultivation was carried out, when Sifnos and its neighbouring islands were able to feed a substantial resident population. Today, however, most of the terraces lie neglected, as the local people prefer to work in the tourist industry.

From the ecological point of view, most of the interest is focused on the peak of Profitis

2 Ilias and its slopes which descend towards the west coast. This whole area is covered with scrub and in places there are limestone cliffs.

The visitor will occasionally come across copses of Phoenician juniper (Juniperus phoenicea) which have over the years taken on a treelike form, while along the beachfronts oleanders and tamarisks grow, and on the sea floor near the beach, one finds colonies of the familiar grass-like marine plant posidonia (Poseidonia oceanica) which is protected under European law.

The Sifnos region is also a corridor for large numbers of migratory birds who come from Africa in the spring on their way to Europe: birds such as orioles (Oriolus oriolus), European bee-eaters (Merops apiaster), turtledoves (Streptopelia turtur) and many species of waterfowl. There are also the birds which come to Greece to spend the summer, such as sand martins (Riparia riparia), swifts (Apus apus and Apus melba), and others.

Finally, we might mention the rare birds of prey which nest in or travel over these
3 regions, including the peregrine falcon (Falco peregrinus), the Falco subuteo and above all the black falcon (Falco eleonorae). The largest population of the latter nests in the Aegean. Another rarely encountered species is the Milos adder (Macrovipra schweizeri), a poisonous snake which is strictly protected because of its rarity. For all of the above reasons, the Profitis Ilias and western Sifnos have been incorporated into the European Union's NATURA 2000 network as a special priority region.

1, 2. Views of the ravine at Kamares.
3. Part of Sifnos with the characteristic stone walls (petzoules) which the locals have devised so as to make their land more cultivable.

2

MYTH & HISTORY

Mythology

References to Sifnos, and to the origins of its many names, are to be found in the works of ancient writers, as well as in the writings of the great travellers who have visited the island. According to legend, Sifnos was the son of the Attic hero Sounios, and his was the name given to the island. Other versions would have it that the name Sifnos was derived from the adjective sifnos meaning empty, a term bringing to mind the many subterranean galleries of the

Bust of a Caryatid and detail (right) from the southern section of the metope on the Treasury of the Siphnians at Delphi. The Delphi Archeological Museum.

mines beneath the island. Pliny says that Sifnos was originally known as Akis or Merope. Other names attributed to it are Sifano, Sifana or Sifanto.

There are a number of different theories about the island's prehistoric inhabitants. Most of the ancient historians are in agreement that Sifnos was first inhabited by the Pelasgians and then by Phoenicians, Carians and Leleges. According to Greek myth, these inhabitants were driven out by Minos, king of Crete, who proceeded to install his sons as leaders of the Cyclades. Stephanos the Byzantine made reference to a town called "Minoa" existing in

Sifnos at that time, and to a spring or fountain of Minoa. The location of both these places remains, however, unknown to this day.

Recent scientific research has come to the conclusion that the entire Aegean was inhabited at that time by a single Mediterranean people, the pre-Hellenes or Aegeans. This people later became intermingled with the Cretans during the period of Minoan supremacy and with the Achaeans during the Mycenaean years.

Neolithic era

When speaking of the Neolithic Era we are referring above all to the economic but also the cultural stage of human development whose cardinal features were the practice of agriculture and stockbreeding.

Chronologically this era covers the long period from 7000 BC to around 2800 BC and is subdivided for practical reasons into the pre-ceramic period, corresponding to the seventh millennium BC, the early Neolithic (sixth millennium BC), the middle Neolithic (fifth millennium BC) and the late Neolithic (4000-2800 BC) periods.

The oldest traces of human habitation that have so far come to light in the Cyclades date from the end of the fifth millennium BC. One of the oldest known settlements in Europe developed in the Aegean during that period. Important factors contributing to the establishment of these early Cycladic settlements were their key geostrategic position in the wider area of the Aegean and the mildness of the climate. At that time people lived in huts made of straw or bricks and subsisted from fishing, hunting and stockbreeding. The oldest finds come from the settlement on Saliagos, a small island near Antiparos. Traces of a fortified village have been found there with a simple enclosure wall dating from the beginning of the late Neolithic period.

Early Cycladic civilisation

The Neolithic period was succeeded by the Early Bronze Age (civilisation of Kephala, Kea, circa 3200 BC). During the subsequent period a very specific form of civilisation evolved in the Cyclades, developing in parallel with the Early Helladic civilisation of mainland Greece and the proto-Minoan of Crete. This was the Early Cycladic civilisation, the study of which got under way following the excavations carried out by the celebrated Greek archaeologist Christos Tsoundas in the years 1898 and 1899. The Early Cycladic civilisation covers the whole of the third millennium BC and is subdivided into three major phases.

The first phase covers the period 3200-2800 BC, the second the period 2800-2200 BC and the third the period 2200-2000 BC, all approximately.

On almost all Cycladic islands, archaeologists have brought vestiges of small settlements to light, chiefly in coastal locations, which were small-scale autonomous communities not subject to any central authority. Their members were related chiefly by blood and their life was substantially linked to the sea. One important fact about them that has been confirmed was the exchange of cultural goods that went on between these small communities and the regions around the Aegean. On Sifnos, Tsoundas brought to light clusters of graves and the foundations of settlements at Akrotiraki near Platis Yialos, at Vathi and at Froudi near Kalamitsi. These graves date from the second half of the third millennium BC.

In particular the prehistoric cemetery at Platis Yialos, where Pollack started investigations in 1896, furnished significant information about the burial customs, grave types and rituals of the islanders of that era. The funeral gifts left beside the dead and brought to light by the exploration of the graves, yielded invaluable data about the stylistic and decorative trends of the time. The finds included earthenware and marble objects such as compasses, food bowls, incised ornaments, bottles and flasks, statuettes, etc.

These archaeological finds opened the way for the study of the economic conditions prevailing on the island. Thus, it was corroborated that Sifnos was then the site of particularly well-developed mining activities centred chiefly around the extraction of silver and lead. Traces of this activity have been detected at Ayios Sostis, Ayios Silvestros, and Xero Xylo. Recent scientific studies also confirm that Sifnos was the most important source for the supply of minerals in the early Bronze Age.

Middle Cycladic civilisation

During the period of the so-called Middle Cycladic Civilisation, which covers the period between 2000/1900 and 1550 BC, life proceeded without any major upheaval. On most of the islands of the Cyclades, excavations have brought to light remains of Middle Cycladic habitations. On Sifnos, the site of a small settlement was identified at Kastro, as indicated by the items of pottery found in the course of the excavations there. Almost all Middle Cycladic settlements, whether coastal or located a short distance inland, relied on farming and on playing an intermediary role in the trade being carried out between the powerful Cretan civilisation and mainland Greece.

Ruins from the acropolis of Ayios Andreas and the church of the same name.

The seafaring Minoan empire in the Aegean was catalytic for the Cyclades. The historian Thucydides mentioned the establishment of Cretan colonies on the islands and, regarding Sifnos in particular, Stephanos the Byzantine reports that there was at that time a city with the revealing name of "Minoa", the location of which has not yet been identified. Minoan supremacy in the entire region at that time was undisputed. The naturalist viewpoint visible in the decorative style of the time simply serves to confirm this influence.

Vestiges of an imposing acropolis survive to this day on the summit of the Ayios Andreas mountain in the southern part of the island. Excavations carried out there by archaeologist Barbara Philippaki indicated the possible existence of a small settlement dating from the beginning of the third millennium BC. It is certain that the site was occupied during the Middle Cycladic period (see p. 92).

Late Cycladic civilisation
(Mycenean Period 1580 - 1100 BC)

In the meantime the Achaeans, who spread throughout the Aegean at the beginning of the second millennium BC, brought the new order that succeeded the age of Minoan rule. The destruction of the Minoan centres around the middle of the millennium helped to strengthen the Myceneans and to consolidate their control throughout all domains. By the late 13th century BC, the Mycenean civilisation had become the new power in the Eastern Mediterranean basin. Mycenean remains have been identified at a number of sites on Sifnos, chiefly at Froudi near Kalamitsi, on the acropolis of Ayios Andreas and at the acropolis of Ayios Nikitas in the north of the island. According to Philippaki, the establishment of the acropolis of Ayios Nikitas dates from Mycenean times.

Archaic period

The year 1125 BC marks the beginning of a new period in Greek history with tribes related to the Achaeans moving down from the mountains to the plains. These migratory movements went on for some three hundred years and played a key role in shaping new conditions.

Between 1130 and 1120 BC, a new group of colonists, the Ionians, came to Sifnos as they did to all of the Cyclades. The leader of the island's Ionian colonists, according to tradition, was Alcenor. The arrival of the new settlers initiated a new phase which was marked, on the one hand, by the need for peaceful and secure living conditions for the inhabitants, on the other by a concerted attempt to deal with the new housing requirements. Thus it was at that time, according to Herodotus, that the new capital of Sifnos was established, the asty or city, in the middle of the eastern side of the island, where present-day Kastro is situated. The new city on the site of an older settlement began slowly to spread and by the 6th century an enclosure wall was being built, while at the centre of the acropolis a temple was being constructed of stone. Excavations carried out by the British Archaeological School (1934-1938) uncovered the remains of buildings and graves from the 8th century BC, which testify to the uninterrupted habitation of Kastro. In the 6th century BC, the old stone temple was rebuilt in marble; new housing was erected at the same time, water-supply and drainage problems were tackled and the city was beautified with new marble buildings including monumental public edifices such as the Prytaneum, the Agora and various sanctuaries. Evidence from the cemetery discovered outside the town makes it clear that the site was in continual use from the 7th century BC until Roman times and later. Archaeological excavations succeeded in locating two marble buildings in the town, one where the church of Ayios Antonios now stands. But the sites of the splendid Prytaneum and Agora, which according to Herodotus had been built of Parian marble, have not been found. Pieces of marble from different objects such as inscriptions, grave stelai, capitals, bases of columns, urns etc. have been found and testify to the highly developed artistic and cultural character of the town.

At the same time the Sifnians fortified the defensive walls of the acropolis (Ayios Andreas). As for the administrative regulations governing the island in historic times, little information is available. The internal organisation must have been the same as that of the Athenians, i.e. there was a king and a senate and later the Eponymous Archon or ruler, the Boule or parliament and the Ekklesia tou demou or assembly.

The people of the island, at that period, afforded particular reverence to the gods Apollo Enargus, Artemis Ecbateria, Zeus Epibemius, Dionysus, Pan, Athena and the Nymphs. The chief occupations of the inhabitants revolved around agriculture, stockbreeding and pottery-making. But metallurgy was the most important. The island's mineral wealth was the most significant factor opening up the greatest prospects for its economic prosperity and cultural development.

The 6th century BC was the Golden Age for Sifnos. Herodotus notes that the Sifnians were "in fact wealthy islanders", which is to say they were the richest islanders, because of the deposits of gold and silver found there. Modern archaeological research has brought to light only the silver mines, at Ayios Sostis in the northeast of the island, which were first worked by the island's prehistoric inhabitants. The latest research confirms that these mines were in fact flooded and -as tradition has long maintained- that the land subsided.

It is indicative of the island's great wealth that coins were minted on Sifnos from around 600 BC, later than Aegina but before Athens and Corinth. Economic prosperity elevated the Sifnians socially as well. The miscellaneous gold, silver, copper, and ivory objects discovered during excavations, and above all the jewellery, are specimens of uncommon elegance.

Ancient columns, grave stelai and casks are visible in the lanes of Kastro among the modern architectural shapes.

But the most important, best known structure created by Sifnos, an indisputable witness to its elegance and prosperity, is the Treasury of the Siphnians, built by the islanders in the sanctuary of Apollo at Delphi. It was constructed in about 525 BC and, according to Pausanias, was financed from a tithe on the profits derived from the gold mines of Sifnos. It was a beautiful building in the Ionian order, which instead of columns had two caryatids on the façade supporting the entablature, with a wealth of exquisitely modelled ornamentation, and a frieze decorated with masterful bas-reliefs running around the treasury on all four sides, totalling 29.63 metres in length. The whole building was 8.55 m. long x 6.12 m. wide and such of its remarkable sculptures as have been saved, which are exceptional examples of mature archaic plastic art, are on exhibit in the Museum of Delphi. This splendid edifice made such an impression that the priestesses at the Delphic sanctuary attributed special honours to the Sifnians for their contribution. Every year the Sifnians sent as their tithe a solid gold egg made from the metal they extracted from their mines.

In the age of the island's greatest prosperity (in the 6th and 5th centuries BC) there were three great acropolises: at the sites of Kastro, Ayios Andreas and Ayios Nikitas. It was at this time that many watch-towers were built at prominent locations on different hills, used as signalling stations for transmitting messages, as lookouts and as a refuge for the islanders in the event of enemy raids. These towers were linked to the three citadels, as well as to the acropolis located in the middle of the island on its highest mountain (now Profitis Ilias), which was the strategic centre for the reception and

transmission of messages. Up to the present, fifty-five signalling towers have been recorded and studied, dating from the 6th to the 3rd century BC. The first attempt at compiling a catalogue of these ancient towers was made by the Sifnian archaeologist Iakovos Dragatsis, who identified thirty-eight of them. But the most comprehensive and detailed record of these towers is to be found in the excellent study entitled: *Sifnos*, Ancient Towers of the pre-Christian Era, *by N. Ashton and E.T. Pantazoglou (Athens, 1991).*

In 524 BC, fugitives from the island of Samos arrived on Sifnos with peaceful intentions. They were political opponents of Polycrates, the demonic tyrant of Samos, and requested financial assistance from the Sifnians in the order of ten talents. The Sifnians refused and so the Samiots, by means of siege and pillaging, forced them to hand over the huge sum of 100 talents. The decline of Sifnos can be dated from this event. It is worth pointing out that when, some years earlier, the Sifnians asked the oracle at Delphi how they might retain possession of their wealth, they received the following answer: "When on Sifnos the Prytaneum and the precinct around the Agora turn white, (i.e. of white marble), then a wise leader will be needed to protect the people from the wooden regiment (i.e. the enemy vessels) and the crimson herald", (i.e. the ambassadors who had boarded a red-coloured ship).

Treasury of the Siphnians.
The Delphi Archaeological Museum.
    1. Four-horse chariot from the south frieze.
    2. Gutter spout with lion's head.
    3. Section of the north frieze.

3

Classical and Hellenistic era

The end of the 6th century BC was marked in Asia by the rise of the Persians, who proceeded to build an immense empire. Their conquest of the Greek cities of Asia Minor and the uprisings of the latter against them brought the first clashes between Greeks and Persians and triggered the two Persian incursions against Greece which followed. In 480 BC, at the naval battle of Salamis, the Sifnians participated with a pentecontoros (i.e. a ship with fifty oars and an eighty-man crew), and at the battle of Plataea in 479 BC, they sent a division of lightly-armed infantry. After the victory at Plataea the Greeks dedicated a golden tripod to the Pythian Apollo at Delphi. On it were engraved the names of the cities which had fought in the war; Sifnos was among them.

In the year 478/77 BC the first Athenian alliance was formed, known as the Delian League. Athens was in a position of leadership and assumed command of the League's navy, establishing the headquarters of the alliance in Delos. Sifnos, like other cities, was a participant and paid an annual tribute for having its autonomy safeguarded by the Athenians. Gradually the ascendance of Athens made itself felt in every sector of public administration, social life and artistic expression, leading to the establishment of a democratic polity on Sifnos as elsewhere.

In 431 the Peloponnesian War broke out between Greece's two powerful city-states: Athens and Sparta. The war spread throughout Greece. According to Thucydides, Sifnos took part in the Athenian expedition against Sicily in 415 BC. In 411 BC, Peisandros imposed an oligarchic polity on Sifnos and 404 BC saw the capitulation and surrender of the Athenians to the Spartans. A pro-Spartan leadership established itself in Sifnos, imposing crippling taxation which aimed at keeping power and control in the hands of the Spartans.

A turbulent period ensued, marked by a succession of political systems on the island. In the meantime a new danger had appeared to threaten the deeply divided Greeks, ruined by decades of internal conflict. The coming of Philip II to the throne of Macedonia in 359 BC radically transformed the balance of forces on Hellenic territory.

Following the victory at Chaeronea in 338 BC and the triumph of Philip, almost all the cities united together in 337 BC in the Corinthian League, which theoretically safeguarded their autonomy but in practice put them under the domination of the king of Macedonia. The same regime was maintained by Philip's successor, his son Alexander. Owing to its strategic position, Sifnos became a meeting place and the site of intense deliberations on a number of occasions. In 334 and 333 BC the Persian fleet under Datamis sailed into Sifnos for the purposes of creating a diversion for Alexander. The enterprise failed, however, after a surprise attack by the Greek fleet under Proteas.

After the death of Alexander the Great in 323 BC all the Cyclades came under the dominion of his successors, initially the Antigonids and then the Ptolemies of Egypt. In these years life went on as normal, with -according to the archaeological evidence- the Sifnians devoting themselves to the construction of fortifications.

The peace was interrupted in 202 BC owing to the desire of Philip V of Macedonia to control the entire Aegean. The friendly relations he maintained with Rhodes made it impossible for him to risk an open clash, so he resorted to striking at it and at other islands by encouraging pirates to raid them. The activity of the pirates dealt a heavy blow to the economy of the islands and the war which broke out between Cretans and Rhodians drove the latter to turn to Rome. At the Isthmian Games in 196 BC, the Romans announced the liberation of Greece. In 162 BC the defeated Cretans attacked Sifnos town but were successfully warded off. They then requested that the Sifnians should permit them to make a peaceful landing on the island. The Sifnians allowed themselves to be persuaded and let them disembark on the island, but the Cretans immediately started looting the town, causing significant damage.

The Roman era

In the meantime a new power was on the rise in Hellenic lands. With the conquest of Corinth in 145 BC by the Romans, Greece became part of the Roman Empire. This was a period of calm in the Cyclades, with the region experiencing an economic boom as a result of growing trade. The Roman Senate proclaimed the harbour of Delos a free port, making it into a centre for trade, and thus favourable economic conditions were obtained for all the islands of the Cyclades. In the first century AD the Mithridatic War broke out between Rome and Mithridates VI, king of Pontus.

The peaceful routine of everyday life was then shattered by violent disturbances. Throughout this period, the islands were plagued by ceaseless pirate raids. In the last years of Roman rule most of the islands had become depopulated or were transformed into places of exile for Romans. Very little information about Sifnos has come down to us from this time.

The Byzantine period

Few reports or written testimonies are extant relating to the course of developments on Sifnos during the Byzantine period. From 324 AD, Sifnos is reported to have been included, along with the other Cycladic islands, in the "Province of the Islands" of the Byzantine state of East Rome, with its capital in Rhodes. At that period, and in the following century as well, Greece and the wider region were shaken by a number of powerful earthquakes as well as by barbarian raids. Chroniclers mention the widespread plague epidemics that ravaged the inhabitants of the Cylades in the 6th century AD. In that century, Sifnos belonged to the 29th Province of the Islands, with its capital at Rhodes. Then the church in Sifnos belonged to the diocese of Paros-Sifnos-Amorgos.

Wall painting of the temple from the Byzantine church of Ayios Sozontos at Apollonia (before Ayios Spyridonas).

The chapel of Panayia Poulati at Yialiskari.

Icon from the temple of Ayios Ioannis Theologos at Kastro.

Despite all the best efforts by the archaeologists who brought to light early Christian religious objects and the ruins of Byzantine buildings, it is not known when Christianity arrived on Sifnos. We do know that by the 4th century AD it had spread over all of Greece.

In the 7th century AD, the Aegean was convulsed by a succession of terrible raids, mainly by Arabs and Slavs, a situation which continued through the subsequent centuries. The new administrative division of the Byzantine Empire into "themes", carried out in the second half of the 7th century, put Sifnos in the theme of the Aegean Sea, with its capital at Samos. It remained in this theme until the first half of the 10th century.

Sifnos could not avoid being drawn into Iconoclastic Controversy. In the 8th century AD, the Cyclades, like all of Greece, revolted against the Emperor Leo III Isaurian (726 AD), but the rebel fleet was ultimately routed.

Through the 11th and 12th centuries the islands frequently fell prey to raids and catastophic sackings by Arab and Latin pirates. In the 12th century the Doge of Venice Domenicus Michelis invaded the Aegean, committing many atrocities. This lawless situation did irreparable damage to the Byzantine state, paving the way for the next visitors from the West, the Crusaders.

The Franks

The fall of Constantinople to the Franks in 1204 led to a redistribution of the territories of the Empire. According to the chronicler Daniel Barbaro, the islands were occupied by the Venetians, who decided to hand them over to private citizens. In 1207, Marco Sanudo, nephew of the Doge of Venice, occupied seventeen islands including Sifnos, establishing the Duchy of the Aegean. Sanudo made Naxos the capital of his island empire and he and his dynasty governed their possessions under the title of the dukes of Naxos or dukes of the Archipelago. In 1279 Sifnos was conquered by the Byzantine admiral Likarios and remained a Byzantine possession until a new situation arose in 1307. In that year Sifnos was captured by Giannoulis Da Corogna, a Spanish knight who belonged to the order of the Knights of St. John. Da Corogna proclaimed his autonomy from the Duke of Naxos and appointed himself independent ruler of the island after first resigning from his order.

The Da Corogna family's period of rule was marked by continual attacks by the Duke of Naxos and the Venetians aiming at recapturing the island and restoring their rule. At the same time a new peril appeared in the Aegean in the form of Turkish pirates, who overran the islands, decimating their populations. When Francisco Crispo came to the ducal throne of Naxos in 1383, the Venetians attempted to deal with the scourge of Turkish piracy, but to no avail.

A description of this turbulent period has been provided by the Florentine monk Christopher Buondelmonti, who travelled around the Cyclades at that time and experienced at first hand the widespread and appalling destitution that prevailed.

In 1464, with the death of the last Da Corogna, Sifnos came into the possession of Nicolo II Gozzadino, of the dynastic family of Kea. He married Marietta Da Corogna, heiress to the island of Sifnos. This marked the successful unification of the two houses of Gozzadino and Da Corogna, with the Kastro on Sifnos designated as the seat of the new state.

The period of government by the Gozzadini was one of the utmost difficulty for the island. During this period, hostilities between Turks and Venetians were an everyday event and Sifnos, like the other islands, had its population greatly reduced. The rule of the Gozzadino family lasted until 1537, when Nicolo Gozzadino became a tributary of the Turkish sultan, paying an annual tax of 300 ducats so as to forestall the loss of his state and/or its destruction at the hands of the notorious pirate Khayr ed-Din Barbarossa.

From then on the Gozzadini continued to rule as vassals of the sultan until 1566, when Sultan Selim II appointed a Jewish bey, a favourite of his named Joseph Nazis, bestowing on him the governorship of the islands. Nazis never went to the islands but administered them through his representative Francisco Coronelo, in accordance with the customs of the islanders, until his death in 1579. The Gozzadini then returned to power in Sifnos, retaining their position by means of various concessions, until 1617, when the Latin dynasts were expelled for good and their tiny state came under the control of the Ottoman Empire, thus inaugurating the period of Turkish rule.

The period of Turkish rule

Following the conquest of the Cyclades by the Turks in 1537, a new political and administrative situation came into being. Valuable information about the institutions of self-government on the islands can be found in the Sultan's surviving decrees of privilege, the so-called ahtnamedes. Most important of all were the ahtnamedes of Chios, which served as the model for those issued later with respect to the Cyclades. They were published during the reign of the sultan Murat III in 1580 and Ibrahaim in 1646 and renewed the special privileges of the islands, including Sifnos. The privileges that were granted, such as permission to rebuild ruined churches, suspension of the custom of taking a male child from each family, recognition of "arbitration" between Greeks, etc., lead to the conclusion that during the period of Turkish rule, the Greeks possessed at least an organised civic authority which devoted itself to obtaining as many privileges as possible for the inhabitants of the islands. According to the ahtnamedes, up to the beginning of the 17th century the islands were administered by a bey who was in turn appointed by the Sultan. However, fear of pirate raids forced the beys to leave the islands and, in the course of their peregrinations, to administer them from wherever they happened to be. It was because of this situation that local government developed on all of the islands. Every year the inhabitants of each island elected the village elders or notables, who had their seat in the capital of the island and had centralised all powers in their hands. They were also charged with collecting the taxes, which they then handed over annually to the Kapudan Pasha (Admiral of the Turkish Fleet) under normal circumstances, or when he was on tour in the islands. On each island there was a cadis (judge) who was usually not a permanent resident, as well as kantzilie-rides, who were like secretaries and were elected either by the inhabitants or by the notables.

Economic recovery got underway in the islands around the middle of the 16th century and it seems that Sifnos was an important commercial centre in the Cyclades from early in the 17th century. Many of its inhabitants turned to shipping, while pottery, spinning and weaving, and the manufacture of straw hats also flourished.

It was then that a dynamic personality made his appearance in the public life of Sifnos: wealthy merchant Vassilis Logothetis, a deeply religious, extraordinarily flexible man of multiple talents who had an elevating influence on the political, religious and cultural affairs of the island. He greatly contributed to strengthening the island's economy and embarked on a major programme of building churches, large and small. In 1642 he financed the construction of the monastery of Panayia Vrysiani.

The Orthodox Church in general reorganised itself with admirable vigour on Sifnos. The diocese of Sifnos was established in 1646, with jurisdiction over eleven islands, and from 1625 to 1634 an "upper" school functioned on the island under the direction of two Catholic priests that had been sent by the Vatican, Giacomo della Roca and Domenico della Gramatica. There was also a "middle" school on Sifnos from 1651 to 1664. The crowning achievement in this sharp upward turn in the island's intellectual and cultural development came in 1687 when the Church in Jerusalem donated the Holy Sepulchre's metochion or dependency on Sifnos to be used to establish the so-called School of the Archipelago on the present site of the two churches of Ayios Ioannis Kalyvitis (today the cemetery of Kastro)

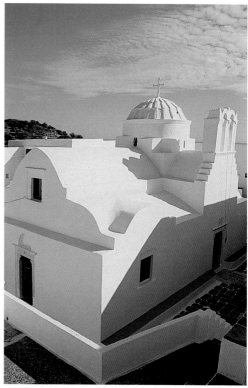

The monastery of Panayia Vrysiani at Exambela.

and Ayios Stephanos, the first martyr. The school, which was staffed with first-rate teachers, included a building complex that served 300 pupils. Some of the most enlightened of the nation's educators taught at it, such as N. Chrysoyelos, E. Trohanis and others; and hundreds of youths graduated from it, then and later, who were to become distinguished men of learning. The School of the Holy Sepulchre functioned until 1835, when it was transferred to the monastery of Ayios Ioannis Chrysostomos (St John Chrysostom), near the village of Kato Petali, and operated as a Hellenic school, an old type of transitional school between elementary and secondary levels, also known as Phyteia. In the meantime, in 1797, the diocese of Sifnos was amalgamated with that of Milos, with its seat at the Kastro of Sifnos.

In the course of the Russo-Turkish War of 1770-1774 the Russians made their appearance in the Aegean, choosing Paros for their base of operations. Sifnos, like the other islands, was occupied at that time by the Orlov brothers. Double taxation was introduced and piracy flourished. At the end of the war, the islands once again returned to Turkish hands. According to travellers visiting the island in those years, the population at the end of the 18th century stood at 4,000 inhabitants. It is worth noting that at that time, in addition to Kastro, a number of other small farming settlements had grown up elsewhere on the island. At the end of the 18th and early 19th centuries conditions were maturing on Sifnos, as they were elsewhere in Greece, for throwing off the Turkish yoke.

Modern times

On 15th April 1821, under the enlightened leadership of the educator Chrysoyelos, Sifnos became an active participant in the struggle for independence from the Turks. Chrysoyelos proclaimed the Revolution on the island, calling all Sifnians to arms. In the years of the Revolution, although there were intense objections to it, chiefly from dignitaries who did not favour the insurgency, the Sifnians distinguished themselves through their actions. Their contribution, especially from the island's monasteries, in terms of both manpower and financial support for the struggle, was invaluable. In 1833, during the regency of King Othon, Sifnos was divided into two municipalities: Apollonia and Artemonas - Kastro. In 1836 these two municipalities were amalgamated into one and the capital was transferred from Kastro to Apollonia.

At the same time, a large number of the inhabitants emigrated, and the island's economy went through hard times. Many Sifnian emigrants achieved great success in different fields of the arts and sciences and always remembered their island, providing it with much needed economic support. Sifnians took part in all the 20th century's major military confrontations, in which, whenever summoned by their country, they served loyally and with all their might in every struggle waged by their homeland for its freedom.

The church of Protomartyras Stephanos (St Stephen) and Ayios Ioannis Kalyvitis.

3

CULTURE & TRADITION

Customs & manners - People & occupations
Arts & letters - Architecture

Many people consider the culture and traditions of a place the most interesting part of any trip, if not its actual raison d'être. Through a people's customs, manners and habits, one becomes aware of the social conditions that shape historic events. From this viewpoint, it would perhaps be more logical for a chapter on culture and tradition to precede the one about the history of the place. We chose to give precedence to history purely for reasons of factual scholarship. In any case the decision about the relative significance of each element is for the reader to make.

Apart from being an island on which Apollo bestowed an abundance of his divine light, Sifnos is also an island with a significant cultural level, and with respect for tradition, customs and manners, an island where cultivating the land became one of the inhabitants' chief occupations, along with fishing. The geological characteristics of the terrain and its rich deposits of clay made it possible for pottery to develop into a true art, which on many occasions helped the island to weather economic storms. In letters too, Sifnos has nurtured distinguished writers,

Quiet moments in the lanes of Sifnos.

folklorists, journalists, educators and jurists, while Cycladic architecture finds perhaps its most consummate expression on this particular Aegean island. Here an immaculate whiteness fills one's entire field of vision as one surveys the scattered cubic volumes found across the length and breadth of the island while the dry stone walls that follow the contours of the terrain, breaking up its surface into horizontal strips, testify once again to the prescience of nature even in architectural matters.

Customs and manners

The island's present-day inhabitants are admirable guardians of the customs and traditions they have inherited from their ancestors. They have assiduously revived all the local customs that link them to the past, emphasising their particularity in the broader Cycladic context, handing them down to their children intact and unadulterated by extraneous influences.

On Sifnos, as on the majority of the islands, most local festivals and social functions are associated with religious and devotional life.

The **feasts** of Sifnos are renowned. They are held in honour of the saints either on the eve of their feast days or on the day itself. The entire organisation and funding of these feasts is taken on by the panegyrades, *that is the family who for a full year keeps the icon of the saint in its house until the day of the feast. On the eve of the saint's feastday, the family lays on a meal for all who have participated. This customary repast is held either in the refectory of the monastery whose feast day is being celebrated or in the open air, if the church concerned is a small one. The basic dish is required to be the traditional chickpea soup, a speciality of the island, but there is also meat. In addition, local wines are served to the accompaniment of abundant toasts to the host or* panegyras, *to the cook and to everyone present. The prevailing atmosphere of good cheer culminates with songs and Sifnian dance music played on the local traditional instruments, the lute and the violin.*

Most visitors will find these feastdays well worth attending as a means of learning something of the island's folk traditions. The most important of these feasts are:

- Panayia tou Vounou (Virgin of the Mountain) on 24th March (eve of the Annunciation).
- Profitis Ilias Psilos and Profitis Ilias Troullakis (Prophet Elijah) on 19th July.
- Saint Panteleimon of Herronissos on 26th July.
- Ayios Ioannis Mavrou Horiou (St John of the Black Village) on 28th August.
- Ayios Ioannis Siderou (St John of the Irons) on 28th August.
- St Symeon the Stylite on 31st August.
- Taxiarchis (Archangel) of Vathi on 5th September.
- Ayios Sostis of the Mines on 6th September.
- Panayia Vrysiani on 7th September.
- Ayios Nikitas on 15th September.
- Ayios Galatis on 5th November.
- Our Lady of the Mountain on 21st November (the Presentation of the Virgin).
- Ayios Andreas (St Andrew) of 29th November.
- Ayios Nikolaos (St Nicholas) on 5th December.
- Panayia Chrysopiyi, on the eve of the Ascension of the Lord. The feast of the Panayia Chrysopiyi is the most important feastday of all, with the entire island taking part, and local and foreign visitors attending.

Another local custom, originating directly from religious life, is that of the traditional Sifnian carols. In Sifnos in the old days, carols were sung only on the eve and on the feastday of St Basil on 1st January. As the great Greek folklorist N.G. Politis reported, Sifnians did not sing a specific carol, but would compose something new every time, reporting the important events of the age, seeking the intercession of the saints, or commenting on persons and incidents. These carols are of exceptional interest both because of their lyrics and their use of the local linguistic idiom, and because of their imaginative original form and content, since they were frequently composed by illiterate people.

Sifnian songs and dances are also of great interest as many have their roots in the distant past. The highly regarded Sifnian scholar and folklorist Antonis Troullos recorded the tradition surrounding an interesting custom,

Festival at Ayia Marina (fig. 1), Profitis Ilias (fig. 2)
and Mavro Horio (fig. 3)

3

People and occupations

The inhabitants of Sifnos are cheerful and kind-hearted; they love their island and are careful to keep up the traditions associated with its history. They are deeply religious people and so the customs, manners and feasts of Sifnos tend to be associated with saints' feastdays. The multitude of beautiful churches on the island also argues in favour of its people's religious spirit; the prevailing architectural order is yet another indication that true faith is found in simplicity.

The Sifnians have their secular side too, of course, and enjoy good food and merry-making; they will initiate you from the very first moment into the secrets of the good Sifnian life, and will delight you with their songs, their local dances and their cuisine, as the island's inhabitants are famous for their cooking abilities and their delicious food. It is not accidental that the famous chef Nikolaos Tselementes, who wrote the classic traditional cookbook found in most Greek homes, is from the Sifnian village of Exambela. Among the island's traditional foods

1. Feast day at the Panayia tis Vrysis Monastery.
2. Sifnian cooking is famous for its traditional chick pea dip ('revithada') which is served on every feast.

the dance of "**Mr North Wind**"; it is an old custom with roots going back to the pagan beliefs prevailing in the pre-Christian years when the people would propitiate the elements of nature that sometimes afflicted them, or would offer them thanksgiving for lenient treatment.

As can be seen from the name, this dance was an expression of joy and thanks to the wind whenever it stopped blowing in the winter, since it usually caused damages and whipped up storms that battered the island. In the 19th century, the dance was performed after vespers on the last Sunday before Lent, in the churchyard of the Panayia tis Conchis in Artemonas. The dance was led first by the priest and then the others would join in; in the old days, the dancers would all be masked.

There were also wonderful Sifnian poems, mainly couplets which were recited as the wine and food were lavishly distributed.

are the famous mastelo *(oven-roast meat) and* revithada *(chickpea soup), which are served at all the restaurants on the island. Among the local sweets, one can single out Sifnian* bourekia, *(little pies),* amygdalota fournou *(oven-baked marzipan),* loukoumia *(Turkish delight) and* pasteli *(a crunchy confection made of caramel and sesame seeds).*

Pasteli, Turkish delight and marzipan are just some of the sweets to be enjoyed at traditional pastry shops of Apollonia and Artemonas.

The island's economy is based primarily on its **agricultural produce**. The most basic products are oil and olives, wine, almonds, onions, capers, figs, sesame seeds, fine thyme-flavoured honey and a few citrus fruits.
A small number of Sifnians are occupied in the breeding of sheep, goats and cattle. The visitor is urged to try the delicious locally-produced cheeses, manoura and myzithra.

Fishing is also fairly well developed and many Sifnians live exclusively from what the sea yields, supplying the island in summer and winter with fresh fish, large and small.

Straw-weaving flourishes on Sifnos, especially the straw hat industry which dates from the years of Latin rule. Textiles are also produced on the island, using the local output of cotton yarns as raw materials.

The people of Sifnos are mainly engaged in primary production occupations.

4

Today, the growing **tourist** trade offers the island a strong financial incentive. In summer particularly, Sifnos is inundated by thousands of people who want to enjoy its attractions. Most of the residents are engaged in tourism-related enterprises and invest more and more time and money in improving the services they provide to visitors. There are quite a few hotels and many apartments to rent. Continuous efforts are being made to improve the island's roads, so that all of its attractions are accessible to everyone. Fortunately the rapidly expanding tourist trade in recent years does not seem to have affected the island's cultural identity, which so much effort has been devoted to protecting.

A primary position in the life of the Sifnians and in the island's economy in general is **pottery**. The geology of the region has contributed to its development, in particular the rich deposits of clay necessary for making pots. Pottery developed greatly during the 19th and early 20th centuries. At the beginning, skilled Sifnian potters concentrated on making functional objects to cover their household needs and the needs of the oil producers, crop and livestock farmers. Thus, utensils used every day were manufactured, such as plates, cups, glasses, pitchers and especially water jars (stamnes) for transporting water, as well as the famous tsikalia, special cooking vessels.

At the beginning, pottery workshops could be found mainly in the island's settlements in the interior, but later, after the War of Independence in 1821, significant pottery workshops sprouted up on seaside sites such as Kamares, Vathi, Platis Yialos, Faros, Herronissos and Seralia Kastrou.

The great love of the Sifnians for the art of pottery (fig. 2, 3), is a source of inspiration for many painters (by K. Kounadis) (fig. 1).

1

2 The craft flourished and the taste of the Sifnians was gradually channelled into artistic creation as well, which resulted in the production of noteworthy pieces. The word "Sifnian" became synonymous with makers of tsikalia and kanates, and with potters more generally. At the same time, the output of this productive activity began to be sold on other markets too, largely by means of maritime trade. Thus began a brilliant period in the export of Sifnian pottery, which enhanced the island's economy significantly. Nor did this craftsmanship remain confined to the island of Sifnos. As time passed, potters increased in number and when their production began to exceed demand the first financial hardships appeared. But there was always demand somewhere, since the craft was now fairly widespread in Greek lands. And so Sifnian potters began to migrate to other regions in which they frequently took up permanent residence. They moved to nearby Cycladic islands and to Thasos, Skopelos, Samos, Lesbos, Chios, 3 Crete and to the islands of the Saronic Gulf. On mainland Greece, they moved to Sparta, Kalamata, Pyrgos Ilias, Thessaloniki, Volos, Halkida, etc. The Sifnians' move to the Attica basin, especially to Piraeus and Maroussi, was particularly productive.

The establishment of Sifnian potters in Maroussi was a collective move of particular interest. Tradition reports that the first potter among the Sifnian craftsmen in Maroussi was named Angelis D. Palaeos.

The names of Sifnian makers of the water jars for transporting water from Maroussi to Athens are well known up to the present time. Since then Maroussi has been the centre of Sifnian pottery.

But apart from the Sifnians who migrated permanently elsewhere, there were also many craftsmen who only left the island seasonally to go to other places, where they would ply their trade and supply the market in summer months, and then in winter would return to their island. Pottery had by then become one of the primary sources of revenue.

Further details and information about Sifnian potters and the dissemination of their craft can be found in the book Oi angeioplastes tis Sifnou ("The potters of Sifnos") by Eleni Spathari-Begliti, Arsenidis Publications and also in the book «Angeioplastiki (traditional pottery) at the island of Sifnos» by Antonis Troulos, 1991. Naturally enough, these migrations initially caused local production to decline. In recent years, though, with the increase of tourist traffic, the demand for Sifnian traditional pottery has increased, and today there are a good many potters' workshops operating on the island at Kamares, Platis Yialos, Herronissos, Vathi and in other villages where lovely local pots are made with names like flari, kanates, stamnes, tsikalia, lainia etc., all with different traditional uses and all products of this unrivalled Sifnian craft.

Examples of Sifnian pottery work with the typical 'flarous' (chimnies) which are used occasionally in the architecture of the island as decorative features..

DEVELOPMENT OF POTTERY ON SIFNOS

Sifnos's 100 pottery workshops (600 potters), which in the old times furnished all of Greece with terracotta cooking vessels, fell into a grave crisis after the war, and were then threatened with extinction. In the 1960s, however, despite the adverse circumstances, a group of officials from the Hellenic Organisation for Small Scale Industries and Handicrafts (EOMMEX) headed by Kostas Kounadis, studied, planned, organised and carried out a pioneering project: the development of Sifnian pottery, a project that relied on local traditional ceramics and was completed within seven years.

The effects of this project (the first of its kind in Greece) were beneficial: the natural environment was preserved and the working and living conditions of Sifnian potters were markedly improved, as were conditions for the population more generally. Sifnos was characterised as a heritage site to be protected, and tourism expanded (especially ecotourism), as did the island's economy.

41

Arts & letters

Sifnos has given Greece some very special people who have distinguished themselves in many different fields of arts, letters and scholarship. With their abundant works and their multidimensional and invaluable contribution, they have supplemented and promoted the cultural identity of their island, opening up new, broader and brighter intellectual horizons.

Nikolaos Chrysoyelos

Nikolaos Chrysoyelos was born in Artemonas, Sifnos in 1780. He attended the School of the Holy Sepulchre and then continued his studies on Patmos and Chios. When he returned to his island in 1808, he was assigned to run the School of the Holy Sepulchre, where he taught and disseminated knowledge to hundreds of young people who later distinguished themselves in public life. At the same time, he became a member of the revolutionary organisation Philiki Etairia, and undertook miscellaneous activities to incite the islanders to rise up and throw off the Ottoman yoke. When the War of Independence broke out in 1821, he was the first to raise the flag of the revolution on Sifnos. He resigned from his position and appointed Nikolaos Sperantsas as his successor at the School. He was placed at the head of an expeditionary force of 150 Sifnians who went first to Hydra, then dispersed onto battlefields and into the Greek navy, where they fought valliantly, imbued with the ideals of liberty. At the same time Chrysoyelos did everything in his power to find financial support for the revolution. In the national assemblies that followed liberation, he was the official representative of Sifnos. In recognition of this outstanding man's contribution, Kapodistrias appointed him Minister of Public Education after liberation, and entrusted him with the Secretariat of Ecclesiastical Affairs. When Kapodistrias was assassinated, Chrysoyelos returned to Sifnos where he was elected three times Mayor, a post he held parallel to his teaching activities.

In 1845 he was sworn in as senator and in 1848 appointed Minister of Education and Religious Affairs under the Kriezis government.

He died in Sifnos on 17 September 1858, leaving a significant body of work behind. Chrysoyelos was the most important cultural and educational figure Sifnos ever produced.

Distinguished Sifnian educators, and writers of poetry and prose

Aristomenis Provelengios (1850-1936): Academician, and one of the most important poets of his time. He wrote lyric poetry and made some important contributions to modern Greek drama. In 1914, he was granted the Arts and Letters Award.

John Gryparis (1870-1942): One of the top modern Greek poets. In 1920 the Academy of Athens awarded him the Arts and Letters Award.

Constantinos Dialismas (1855-1921): Significant educator, graduate of the Great School of the Nation and the University of Athens. He established a private school in Piraeus and later in Athens and was very active in the social and educational fields. He was a prolific author.

Iakovos Dragatsis (1853-1934): A well-known educator and outstanding archaeologist. He established the Dragatseio school and conducted successful excavations as the Ephor of Antiquities in Piraeus. He directed archaeological research and excavations on Sifnos as well. His scholarly publications were significant.

Apostolos Makrakis (1831-1905): Theologian and philosopher with multi-faceted activity. He established a new educational and philosophical school called "School for Discourse" in Athens, the religious association "John the Baptist", and the newspapers Dikaiosyne (Justice) and Logos (Discourse). He left behind him a great wealth of publications.

Nikolaos Ant. Dekavallas (1884-1938): Was awarded a doctorate from the School of Philosophy, University of Athens, with highest honours, and went on to linguistic studies in Germany, Leipsig and Jena. He contributed decisively to compiling the Great Historical Dictionary of the Greek Language, and left behind an enormous volume of writings.

Kleanthis N. Triantafyllos, "Rampagas" (1849-1889): A scintillating and independent spirit, he was one of the greatest satiric poets of his time. In the pages of his newspaper Rampagas, he wrote blistering articles deploring the evils and corruption of his era. His uncompromising spirit brought imprisonment and prosecution upon him. Today, his bust adorns Rampagas Square in Apollonia.

Nikolaos G. Kambanis (1846-1936): Pioneering and militant journalist, with a long catalogue of publications covering his entire life. In 1880 with minimum means, he established the newspaper Sifnos, a valuable source of historical and sociopolitical information about his island. He has left behind a rich cultural heritage in his publishing activity.

The list of famous Sifnian teachers, poets, authors and journalists is a long one, and takes us up to the present day. It includes names such as: Leandros Arvanitakis (1823-1892), Georgios Vionis (1822-1898), Ioannis Valetas (1818-1900), Stelios G. Sperantsas (1888-1962), Theodosis K. Sperantsas (1888-1979), Georgios S. Vernikos (1845-1936), Antonis Prokos (1912-1993), Antonis G. Maganaris-Dekavallas, Nikos G. Stafylipatis, Titos Patrikios, Giorgos Likos, Leandros Polenakis, Julietta Karori, and others.

Distinguished Sifnian authors, archaeologists and folkorists

Manos Th. Philippakis (1912-1985): The most significant scholar of Sifnian folklore. His best known paper was entitled "Place names in Sifnos".

Barbara Th. Philippaki: archaeologist, awarded a PhD from the University of Oxford. Conducted important excavations on Sifnos. In 1969, directed the excavation of the Ayios Andreas acropolis on the island.

Manolis Korres: Playwright with varied activities who has received many awards and has written some enormously successful works.

Antonis G. Troullos: Distinguished scholar with a significant cultural contribution, who has been honoured by the Academy of Athens. To his credit are many worthwhile publications chronicling the historical and folkloric wealth of Sifnos.

Simos Miltiadis Symeonidis: Tireless scholar, researcher and historian, he has been engaged in systematically gathering and recording the rich material from Sifnos. Young scholars are urged to study his work.

Painting of Sifnos by K. Kounadis.

Archimandrite Filaretos Vitalis: Important writer and scholar who has made a valuable contribution to the field of ecclesiastical art and history.

Evangelos Th. Pantazoglou: Received the Academy of Athens award in 1994 for his book Sifnos, Ancient Towers in the pre-Christian Era (Athens 1991), on which he collaborated with Prof. Norman Ashton. Artist, photographer and scholar, he has for years devoted himself to promoting the attractions and history of his homeland.

Also worthy of mention are author Giorgos Theologos-Petalianos (1917-1977), folklorist Victoria Veloutsou (1892-1986), educator Georgios B. Prokos, author of the book Brief History of the Elementary School in Artemonas Sifnos, and scholar and teacher Nikos Kalamaris, author of the study School of the Archipelago, and many others.

There have also been many famous Sifnian jurists: Antonios G. Zilimon (1868-1944), Constantinos G. Provelengios (1800-1880), Antonios K. Romanos, Georgios Ant. Dekavallas (1885-1972), Georgios Soph. Maridakis (1889-1979).

And finally, two publications are worthy of note for their efforts to preserve the Sifnian cultural heritage, while at the same time publicising the current social and cultural activity on the island: the newspaper Sifnos which was established in 1880 by N.G. Kambanis, and the newspaper Sifnaika Nea which was established in 1947 by "Ayios Symeon", the Brotherhood of Sifnians.

Architecture

Sifnos occupies a unique position in the western Cyclades both for its beautiful natural landscape and for its constructed space as well. Cycladic architecture, which is a characteristic feature of most of the islands, and unquestionably unique, can be found here in an absolutely pure form.

Cubic volumes drenched in radiant light are dispersed harmoniously over the hillsides adding an interesting geometric element to scenery of rare beauty. On undeveloped parts of the island, the landscape is accented by dry stone fences that follow the contours of the terrain, breaking up surfaces into successive, almost horizontal strips. Thus many tracts of arable land are demarcated, access to which is by means of paths. Dotted round the countryside are little rural structures, known as themonies. They are inhabited seasonally by farmers working their land. These rural dwellings can be found throughout the islands.

Many of them have some outbuildings; inside them, a necessary feature is the panostria, or fireplace. Somewhere around the themonia is likely to be the aloni or stone threshing-floor, ready for the year's harvest. Also there are a lot of dovecotes near the themonies, at the edge of fields and rocky areas. Those dovecotes adorn the land with their characteristic shapes. Windmills occupy crucial positions near villages, and constitute exceptional examples of vernacular architecture.

The island's traditional settlements are on a plateau inland and constitute a virtually continuous group of seven villages laid out one beside the other. These are the villages of Exambela, Katavati, Apollonia, Pano Petali, Artemonas, Aï Loukas and Kato Petali, the latter of which is set more apart. The settlement of Kastro is on a totally independent site, and more will be said about it in another part of the book (see p.71).

The organisation and evolution of these

1

central settlements dates to the last years
of the period of Turkish rule, taking on a more
complete form in the 19th century, when
Apollonia became capital of the island.
They were planned around a central
pedestrian walkway, which branches out on
both sides into smaller, secondary paths. The
houses are arranged along these secondary
paths in a fairly free but solid way. The image
of the Sifnian constructed environment shows
the simple but striking cubic buildings in sharp
relief. A unique aesthetic value is also
acquired by the attractive, well-kept walks
paved with flagstones with whitewashed
cracks, and low walls on which people
can stop for a rest.

The houses of Sifnos are built largely of
local materials, stone and wood. The local
schist rock or slate has been lavishly used in
masonry. Both inside and out, walls are
plastered with a mixture of sand and
quicklime, giving them the dazzling white
colour characteristic of the Cyclades. An
interesting feature of the houses is the typical
flat roof of the houses (doma).

3

On Sifnos the traditional type of dwelling
prevails, with few variations. Old mansions are
particularly grand, most of which were built by
distinguished residents of the Kastro who had
gone elsewhere, or by other wealthy Sifnians,
either local people or emigrants. These
mansions were built using as a model the
gracious homes on the Kastro, while a good
many of them, dating primarily to the end of
the 19th century, show strong neoclassical
features, which do not however detract from
their traditional style. Inside, they usually
consist of one sitting room and two bedrooms
at the back.

1. *Building works on Sifnos are completed with patience,
   taste and affection.*
2, 3. *Solitary windmills and traditional dovecotes are
   splendid examples of the island's architecture.*

This basic pattern can be encountered in a number of variations with the addition of other auxiliary areas, or additional main areas and bedrooms. The same type of pattern is followed by the island's middle-class houses. Many of the old mansions also have a large, fenced out-door courtyard. An essential feature of Sifnian homes is the courtyard, usually enclosed by a low wall, or the balcony (exostis), which has a direct functional relation with the house. Many houses have the characteristic steadia, i.e. roofed semi-outdoor areas in front of the entrance. In the interior of these homes, attractive lateral vaulted openings called voltes are often used.

The Sifnian home is characterised by great simplicity. Inside there are a many constructed benches, the essential panostria, or fireplace, and the absolutely minimal furniture. Basins are necessary for washing clothes and, of course, cisterns for collecting rainwater.

The picture of the Sifnian home is supplemented by the little stairways that lead inside and the attractive flari, or chimneys. These chimneys are usually made of terracotta; they can be found in various shapes and, apart from their functional use, are a wonderful decorative feature.

More generally, it could be said that the architecture of Sifnos offers rare aesthetic pleasure to the modern visitor.

Church architecture

On Sifnos there are many churches and chapels dotted about the natural landscape. In fact, there is a tradition that there are 365 churches on the island, one for each day of the year. On Sifnos, most of the churches are privately owned, having been built by the island's seamen, among whom it was the custom to build a church in order to secure their salvation.

Simple but impressive, the square-shaped houses highlight the sensitivity of the locals for design, construction and conservation.

One noteworthy feature of the village churches is their absolute incorporation into the community in which they are located.

Most of the churches are dedicated to the Virgin Mary, Christ, St John the Baptist, the Prophet Elijah –who is venerated on mountain tops– to St Nicholas, patron saint of seafarers, and St Sozon.

No churches from the Byzantine period have been preserved on Sifnos, although tradition tells us that the katholikon (main church) of the Monastery of Profitis Ilias and the Panayia Angeloktisti in Katavati are both very old.

The most widespread types of churches are aisleless domed churches and flat-roofed basilicas with either one or two aisles. Inside one finds the usual three-part division into sanctuary, nave and narthex (sometimes used as the women's section, or gynaikonitis); the entrance is usually on the south side. Frequently there are elegant belltowers over

the entrance with pedimental roofs. Church entrances are usually flanked by a marble border and have a marble lintel overhead, often with incised inscriptions. The entrance to the church of Ayios Sozon and Phanourios at Apollonia is typical, with its marble border, cornice and brackets, and its rich decoration.

Most of the churches can be dated to the 16th, 17th and 18th centuries. All are pristine white with simple decoration, and are barely distinguishable from the houses and other buildings in the community.

Some of them have decorative plaques inlaid in their interior walls, like the one in the church of the Taxiarchis in Apollonia, where the plaques on the curved outside façade of the apse form a cross. Inside the churches, the floors are usually made of slate flagstones with the joints whitewashed and are frequently decorated with gravestones, coloured round marble plaques (omphalia) and double-headed eagles. In some places, there are unusual floors with plaques and pebbles worked in geometric shapes and attractive compositions. Domes are not covered with ceramic tiles, but by a coat of whitewash; some may have the deep blue colour characteristic of the Cyclades. Many of them are also pierced by small one-light windows. There is a lovely dome on the church of Panayia Poulati in Dialiskari around the lower part of which is a horizontal cornice enhanced by terracotta acroteria.

The church of Panayia tis Ammou (Virgin of the Sand) in Artemonas is a aisleless flat-roofed basilica, and that of the Metamorphosis tou Sotirou (Transfiguration of the Saviour) in Apollonia a two-aisled flat-roofed basilica. The church of the Timios Stavros (True Cross) in Apollonia belongs to the type of aisleless domed churches. The three-aisled vaulted church of Ayios Constantinos in Artemonas is worthy of note, as each of its arms is covered by a slightly pointed vault, the middle vault being somewhat higher. Another unique type on the island is that of Panayia Angeloktisti ('Angel-built') at Katavati, which belongs to the type of the three-aisled inscribed cross-in-square

1

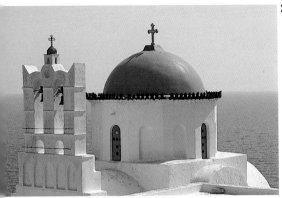

2 church. Almost all churches have an outer courtyard usually located to the south of the building. These churchyards are used for religious ceremonies but also for cultural and social events. Inside the island's churches, the visitor is likely to find marvellous carved wood or marble templa (icon screens). A careful look at these templa will reveal noteworthy old icons, including many examples of Cretan art.

Many outstanding religious painters worked on Sifnos in the 16th, 17th, 18th and early 19th centuries including Emmanuel
3 Skordilis, Constantinos Palaiokapas, Zacharias Tzakaropoulos, the priest-monk Nikiforos of Cyprus, Melisos Nikolaos, the priest-monk Athanasios, Deuterevon of Sifnos, and others, who continued the tradition of Byzantine religious painting and created wonderful works of post-Byzantine art. Although there are wall paintings in just a few churches, they will reward the visitor's effort to see them. Worthwhile wall paintings can be found in the churches of Panayia Gournia in Artemonas, Panayia Angeloktisti in Katavati,
4 Ayios Sozon in Apollonia, Ayios Antypas in Ano Petali, the Taxiarchis tis Skafis and chapel of the Presentation of the Virgin in the church of Ayios Georgios in Katavati.

The monasteries of Sifnos are the trustees and guardians of the island's spiritual heritage and cultural tradition. They are laid out in the traditional pattern with the main church (katholikon) in the centre and with the cells and outbuildings surrounding them. The most important monasteries accessible to the public are: Panayia tis Vrysis, Panayia "to Vouno" (of the mountain), Phyrogia, Ayios Ioannis Theologos Mongos, Chrysostomos, Panayia Chrysopiyi, Panayia Poulati, Profitis Ilias. Access to the Taxiarchis tis Skafis, a dependency of the Monastery of the Profitis Ilias, is not difficult.

1. The church of Ayios Konstantinos in Artemonas. The churches of Sifnos are bathed in the colours of the sky and of innocence.
2. Panayia Poulati.
3. Profitis Ilias.
4. Panayia "to Vouno" (of the mountain).

TOUR OF THE ISLAND

The best way to get to know a place is to start with a well organised tour. To ensure that you have the best possible tour of the beautiful island of Sifnos, we propose two itineraries that we have drawn up for you. The island has been divided in two on the basis of inhabited villages, and our itineraries do not attempt to cover the whole island geographically.

*The **first itinerary** takes you from Kamares to Apollonia, from there to the villages of Katavati, Exambela and Kato Petali, and then heading north it goes to Artemonas, Kastro and Herronissos at the northernmost tip of the island.*

*The **second itinerary** will take you to some of the island's most beautiful monasteries, Panayia "to Vouno" and Chrysopiyi, as well as to the beaches at Faros, Vathi and Platis Yialos.*

CENTRAL & NORTHERN SIFNOS:
*Kamares – Apollonia – Kato Petali –
Katavati – Exambela – Pano Petali –
Artemonas – Kastro – Herronisos*

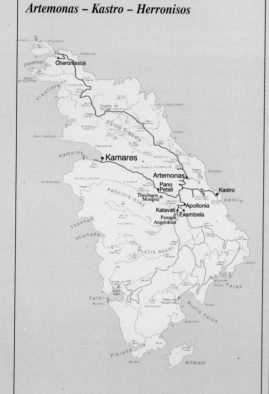

SOUTHERN SIFNOS:
*Monastery of Panayia "to Vouno" –
Monastery of Chrysopiyi – Platis Yialos –
Faros – Acropolis of Ayios Andreas – Vathi*

Sights worth seeing and ...taste :

MUSEUMS
- Archaeological Museum in Kastro (p. 75)
- Ecclesiastical Art and Tradition (p. 65)
- Sifnos Folklore Museum, Apollonia (p. 60)

ARCHAEOLOGICAL SITES-
Acropolis of Ayios Andreas (p. 92)
- Kastro (p. 70)

ΕΚΚΛΗΣΙΕΣ
- Ayia Anna (p. 54)
- Ayia Katerina (Artemonas, p. 68)
- Ayia Katerina (Kastro, p. 76)
- Ayia Katerina (Seralia, p. 78)
- Ayia Marina (p. 54)
- Ayia Sofia (p. 77)
- Ayioi Anargyroi (p. 58)
- Ayioi Pantes (p. 76)
- Ayioi Saranta (p. 76)
- Ayios Andreas (p. 92)
- Ayios Antonis (Kastro, p. 77)
- Ayios Antypas (p. 66)
- Ayios Dimitrios (p. 76)
- Ayios Georgios (Artemonas, p. 68)
- Ayios Georgios (Kamares, p. 54)
- Ayios Georgios (Katavati, p. 62)
- Ayios Ioannis (Ano Petali, p. 66)
- Ayios Ioannis Theologos (p. 74, 76)
- Ayios Ioannis Prodromos (Kastro, p. 76)
- Ayios Ioannis Prodromos (Seralia, p. 78)
- Ayios Konstantinos (p. 67)
- Ayios Nikolaos (p. 76)
- Ayios Spyridon (p. 60)
- Ayios Sozon (p. 60)
- Christos (Kastro, p. 78)
- Christos (Katavati, p. 62)
- Kimisis Theotokou (Dormition of the Virgin, p. 76)
- Metamorphosis Sotiros (Transfiguration, p. 60)
- Panayia tis Ammou (p. 68)
- Panayia Angeloktisti (p. 62)
- Panayia Barou (p. 60)
- Panayia "Gournia" (p. 66)
- Panayia Eleoussa (p. 76)
- Panayis tis Conchis (p. 68)
- Panayia Mangana (p. 79)
- Panayia Ouranafora (p. 60)
- Panayia Poulati (p. 78)
- Panayia Troullakiani (p. 79)
- Profitis Ilias Hamilos (p. 63)
- Protomartyras Stephanos (St Stephen, the first Martyr, p. 78)
- Sotir (Redeemer, p. 78)
- Taxiarchis (p. 60)
- Theoskepasti (p. 76)
- Timios Stavros (p. 60)
- Zoodohos Piyi (Fount of Life) p. 62)

MONASTERIES
- Ayios Ioannis Theologos Moungos (p. 64)
- Chrysopiyi (p. 85)
- Chrysostomos (p. 78)
- Efta Martyres (Seven Martyrs, p. 77)
- Panayia "to Vouno" (p. 84)
- Panayia Vrysis or Kyra Vrysiani (p. 64)
- Phyroyia (p. 63)
- Prophitis Ilias Psilos (p. 63)
- Prophitis Ilias Troulakiou (p. 54)
- Taxiarchis (p. 94)

BEACHES
- Apokoftos (p. 88)
- Dialiskari or Poulati (p. 78)
- Faros (p. 91)
- Phasolos (p. 91)
- Glyfos (p. 91)
- Herronissos (p. 80)
- Kamares (p. 52)
- Platis Yialos (p. 90)
- Saoures (p. 88)
- Seralia (p. 77)
- Vathi (p. 92)

Some of the ancient towers can be visited, such as those at Ayios Haralambos and Ayios Eleftherios and Panayia Anemordyli.

You may also be interested in the traditional pottery workshops at Kamares, Exambela, Platis Yialos, Apollonia and Artemonas.

And finally, you are advised to try traditional foods such as mastelo, chick pea soup and chick pea patties, and local sweets such as marzipan, Turkish delight, halva pie and bergamot orange preserves.

The itinerary includes a visit to the part of Kamares the main town of Apollonia, the villages at Katavati, Exambella, Kato and Pano Petali, Artemonas, the historic settlement of Kastro and the picturesque hamlet of Hersonisos.

Kamares

As the ship approaches the dock, the first thing to meet the eye of the traveller is the slope of two steep hills and the little settlement of Kamares.

The harbour at Kamares, which today provides the only access to the island for people travelling on ships of the line, was initially built in 1907 and then enlarged in 1950. The little village of Kamares around it is comparatively recent, and began to develop around the end of the 19th century. The first image it offers is the familiar Cycladic white dictated by the modern settlements along the coast. On one side is the wharf at which caiques and other boats are moored, and on the other side the village climbs gently up the slopes of the hill. Some of the island's old potters were once located there. The beach at Kamares with its fine sand is one of the most beautiful on the island and offers a variety of activities such as swimming, sea sports and sun bathing, since the water there is usually very calm. The settlement that has spread out behind it is more of a tourist resort. There you can find the community information bureau, various tourist offices and small hotels.
The village also has a good many rooms to let during the summer season.

& NORTHERN SIFNOS

Exambela - Pano Petali - Artemonas - Kastro - Herronisos

Visitors sitting right on the seaside can enjoy fresh fish and seafood in one of the countless tavernas all in a row, or drink a coffee in the little seaside coffee shops and pastry shops (zacharoplastia). For shopping, there are many stores, supermarkets, bookshops, and pottery workshops displaying local folk art wares. In summer the village is humming with life and those who like evening entertainment will find a variety of pleasant bars in the area.

To the left of the harbour is the settlement of **Ayia Marina** with the church of the same name, and **Ayia Anna**, a picturesque little chapel clutching the side of the mountain. At the top of the hill that defines Kamares, you can see the **monasteries of Ayios Symeon** and Profitis Ilias Troullakiou. In the centre of Kamares is the church of **Ayios Georgios**, well worth a visit.

Although Kamares, a busy and hospitable place, guarantees that visitors' first contact with the island is a pleasant one, nothing can prepare them adequately for the variety of beautiful and interesting places to come.

Views of picturesque Kamares.

View of central Sifnos.

Artemonas

Ano Petali

Katavati

Apollonia

The route from Kamares to Apollonia, the capital of the island is over a winding road that takes the traveller away from the sea and across the mountain slopes, gradually revealing all the sculptured beauty of the Sifnian landscape. From the beginning, the visitor is captivated by the dry stone walls that divide the land into almost parallel terraces, and by the countless little paths highlighting the natural environment. These low stone walls, or louria (belts) as the Sifnians call them, simultaneously follow and define the morphology of the terrain. Every so often little dovecotes appear before you, and snow white chapels, an integral feature of the Cycladic architecture.

Taxiarchis - Artemonas

Ayios Loukas

Kamaroti

Apóllonia

Half way along, to the right of the road, in a verdant natural hollow, is the picturesque **church of the Ayioi Anargyroi** (Sts Cosmas and Damian, the "silverless" physicians who frequently refused payment), with its underground crypt and miraculous spring. The distance from Kamares to Apollonia is just 5 km and the road takes you into the heart of Apollonia, to the large village square.

Apollonia, which has been the capital of the island since 1836, owes its name to the cult of Enargus Apollo during the pre-Christian years. Today it is also called Stavri. It is the main village on the island, built amphitheatrically around three hills. Apollonia is the commercial and administrative centre of Sifnos, and the largest number of the island's permanent residents is concentrated here. Its physical layout is defined by a central pedestrian walkway which branches off onto smaller side paths on each side. Visitors will admire its traditional architecture expressed in pristine white cubic dwellings, its flagstone lanes with whitewashed outlines, its flower-bedecked courtyards with low walls, its whitewashed steps, and its picturesque churches with white or sky-blue domes and elaborate belltowers.

Everywhere, simplicity contributes to creating a unique, elegant aesthetic. A stroll through the various neighbourhoods is full of constant surprises and the sight of this wonderful village bathed in brilliant sunlight can hardly fail to move the visitor. In addition to its aesthetic pleasure, Apollonia can also provide all the comforts necessary to ensure a pleasant stay. Picturesque tavernas featuring Sifnian specialities, traditional pastry and coffee shops, stores displaying folk art objects, hotels and rooms to rent, innumerable bars and coffee shops promise days and nights of enjoyment and entertainment. Here too you'll find a post office, banks, chemist's shops, a dentist, a health centre, a police station, many travel agencies and a Folk Museum.

Apollonia: bathed in the light of Apollo.

A walk along the main pedestrian sidewalk will reveal many churches that are integrally linked with and absolutely incorporated into the settlement as a whole. It is worth visiting the **church of the Timios Stavros** (True Cross), a type of shortened, domed cross-in-square church, possibly dating from the 17th century, as well as the **church of the Taxiarchis** (Archangel), of the same architectural type, which has plaques inlaid on the outer wall of the apse and over the entrance, and a marvellous templon (icon screen). As you proceed, you'll encounter the two-aisled flat-roofed basilica dedicated to Ayios Athanasios and the **church of the Metamorphosis tou Sotiros** (Transfiguration of the Saviour), another two-aisled flat-roofed basilica with two splendid icon screens. Another aesthetic treat is provided by the **church of Ayios Sozon** with its fine wall paintings and the **church of Panayia Barou**. Walking up the main street, after Rambayas Square, one's attention is drawn to the **cathedral of Ayios Spyridon** on the left which was remodelled in 1901.

On the other side of Apollonia, the **church of Panayia Ouranofora or Geraniofora** is also worth seeing, on which the date 1767 has been preserved, when the church was refurbished. It was very likely built on the ruins of an ancient temple, in whose courtyard the Lolopaneyiro, a frenzied feast with abundant food, drink, dancing

and singing, used to take place on 2 February.

In the main square of Apollonia is the war memorial (Iroon) and the Sifnos **Folklore Museum** which has been open since 1974.

In this museum are some exhibits that bear living witness to the high level of Sifnian folk art and cultural heritage. Inside, to the left of the entrance and up a small stairway, is a hall in which a variety of items are exhibited, including guns and swords belonging to Sifnian fighters, booty from battles, nautical instruments, handmade tools from assorted occupations such as a goldsmith's bellows, a one-cylinder steam engine, a wood lathe, and others. Hanging on the wall are pages from the newpaper Sifnos, which has been published continuously from 1880 up to the present. There is also a list of Sifnian patriarchs and archbishops up to 1923 and busts of famous Sifnians such as N. Chrysoyelos, Apostolis Makrakis, and others.

In the second hall to the right and in the intermediate corridor, stones are displayed from the acropolis of Ayios Andreas, an earthenware cauldron lid, a Sifnian foot-powered potter's wheel, a barrel, a kopanos or skourlos (mallet for breaking up potter's clay) and various other potters' tools. One can also see objects such as a brazier for warming a room, a clay soup pot, a vase with nozzle, a cooking pot (tsikali), various earthenware containers, plates, terracotta stamnes (pitchers), a basket for collecting olives, a wooden loom tool, various pottery food platters (one bearing a painted image of King George II and dated 1936), earthenware oil jars, pitchers and cooking pots. Likewise on display are a carved wooden trunk, a handmade wooden hobbyhorse, accessories from a Sifnian loom, the base of a scale with hollows for pans, face towels of Sifnian textiles, head kerchiefs, wooden distaffs, wooden coffee mill, loom implements and various other functional utensils.

In the first hall are the vestments of Metropolitan Polycarp Synodinos of Messinia, the outfit of a Sifnian elder made of loom-

2 woven fabric, a copy of a Sifnian women's costume (in memory of Oli - Antoniou - Troulou), various handmade items and articles of clothing such as an embroidered tablecloth, men's and women's clothing (19th century), knitted socks (tsourapia), lace neckwear, Sifnian bobbin lace, lace-trimmed pillowcase, bridal cushion cover from 1904, woven blankets and carpets, shawls, a bridal outfit, embroidered combcase, etc.

3 And finally there is a wooden display case in which you can find copies of various Sifnian newspapers, and above all a collection of books by Sifnian authors that have been published up to the present time. Sifnian folklorist Antonios Troullos made a significant contribution to ensuring that the exhibition is as complete as possible and that the space is utilised in the most efficient way.

1. The cathedral of Ayios Spyridon in Apollonia.
2, 3, 4. Views from the Folklore Museum.

4

Kato Petali, Katavati, Exambela

From Apollonia, a path leads to the village of **Kato Petali**. But there is also a paved road leading there from the capital, just 1.5 km away. When the visitor sees the village from afar, it seems to be standing proudly on a hill in the lovely Sifnian landscape. The village is built around a central square paved with stone, in which stands the pretty **church of Zoodochos Piyi**, with its tower-like steeples. There is also a fairly modern carved marble icon-screen inside the church. The architecture of the village repeats the Cycladic motifs and the settlement in its entirety offers yet another hospitable corner for the visitor.

By following Apollonia's ascending main walkway, visitors will find themselves in the village of **Katavati**, a continuation of the capital. The philosopher and theologian Apostolis Makrakis was a native of Katavati. It is his bust that adorns the village square that also bears his name. On the way, the visitor will encounter one of the prettiest churches on the island, **Panayia Angeloktisti (Angel-built)**. This is a three-aisled cross-in-square church.

The hemisphere of its cupola is covered by a conic dome that rests on a high cylindrical drum. On the interior, the floor of the church is decorated with plaques and pebbles, while in the centre there are two pebble mosaics of double-headed eagles, one below the other, the colours of which have been preserved fairly well. On the north wall of the main church is an inlaid bas-relief marble slab that depicts the figures of Sts Constantine and Helena holding between them the True Cross of the Lord. The walls of the church are covered with attractive paintings by an anonymous folk artist, but they need conservation.

Other noteworthy churches in the village are **Christos** (Christ Church) and **Ayios Giorgios** (St George) which is a aisleless triconch church; it has a chapel of the Presentation of the Virgin with painted decoration on both its conchs. A little farther up, at the edge of the village, is the **church of Prophitis Ilias Hamilos** (= Low). It is so named in contrast with the **monastery of the Prophitis Ilias Psilos** (= High) which is on the island's highest peak.

On the highest peak of Sifnos is the **monastery of the Profitis Ilias Psilos**, as it is called, which according to tradition is one of the oldest buildings on the island. The winding path that starts above Katavati leads up to the monastery and can only be travelled on foot, a fairly tiring uphill walk of about an hour and a half. On the monastery site, as confirmed by the archaeologist I. Dragatsis, traces can be seen of the foundations of a large ancient structure which has not as yet been dated. It is probably a large citadel inside which was an ancient temple.

According to tradition, the main church (katholikon) of the present monastery dates back to the eighth century, although there is no evidence to support this hypothesis. The earliest date to have been preserved on an inscription is 1145. The fact is that in a patriarchal document dated 1654, the monastery is reported as being under construction. The present complex is surrounded by stout walls, and consists of the katholikon, a large refectory, underground galleries reminiscent of catacombs, basement rooms under the monastery floor, cells all around for the accommo-

dation of visitors, and a church dedicated to Ayios Elissaeos which is situated outside the walls and bears an inscription dated 1749. The katholikon of the monastery does not have the characteristic features of Byzantine Cycladic architecture. It is a tetrastyle cross-in-square church with five domes that has obviously gone through many restorations. On the interior there is a marble templon and a marble baptismal font.

The feastday of this monastery is celebrated on the eve of the feast the Prophet Elijah (20 July) and is attended by many people. Visitors walk up to the monastery in the afternoon of 19 July, eat a meal there consisting of the traditional chickpea soup, celebrate all night long with traditional Sifnian songs, and then after attending the early morning festive service, return home.

The monastery of the Prophitis Ilias is not inhabited today, although in the past it had a large number of monks. In winter the monks would usually descend to the **monastery of Phyroyia**, a dependency of the Profitis Ilias.

The old monastery of Phyroyia is about one km from Katavati and was dedicated to Ayios Athanasios and the Presentation of the Virgin Mary. Today's visitor can see the main church, which is a domed basilica, a few cells and the high stone wall that surrounds it. Some incised inscriptions and dates have been preserved that testify to the history of the monastery over the ages. Otherwise, there are few accounts relating to Phyroyia, although it is known that Anthimus, the Sifnian Metropolitan of Belgrade, resided there for a period of time.

2

1. *Kato Petali.*
2. *Thorough preparation and large-scale participation characterise the feast at the monastery of the Profitis Ilias Ypsilos.*

Another important monastery just outside Apollonia, at the foot of the Profitis Ilias mountain, is that of **Ayios Ioannis Theologos Mongos** (St John the Divine, the "Mute"). It was once a convent that initially belonged to the Diocese of Sifnos and in 1655 was elevated to a stavropegion, i.e. was directly attached to the Ecumenical Patriarchate in accordance with a sigillio issued by the Sifnian Ecumenical Patriarch Ioannikos II, which has been preserved in the manuscript section of the National Library. In 1834, the convent was disbanded by the Bavarian government.

The katholikon of the monastery, which is one of the most important post-Byzantine monuments on the island, is a aisleless domed basilica. The cells around it have undergone a large-scale renovation. On the lintel of the church's main entrance is the family crest of the Italian family of Gozzadino. The right hand bell bears the date 2[September 1508 in Latin, a particularly important piece of information indicating that the church was built at the beginning of the 16th century and perhaps even earlier, if we accept that the bell tower is a later structure. Inside the katholikon, the visitor can admire the superb carved wood gilt templon, a masterpiece of the 17th century. The icons that adorn it were created by the significant Cretan artist Emmanuel Skordilis. Of particular importance is the icon of St. John the Divine which very likely dates to the 15th century. In the interior of the church there is an icon-stand and episcopal throne from the 18th century, as well as an altar with ciborium.

The little settlement of Eleimonas, on a site with a superb panoramic view, is an extension of **Katavati**. Leaving Katavati behind, the visitor will pass the Arades, a group of symmetrically arrayed windmills, heading in a southeasterly direction toward the village of Exambela, the birthplace of the Sifnian poet and Academician Aristomenis Provelengios, and of the famous chef Nikolaos Tselementes. Provelengios's house at the entrance to Exambela is a well-kept mansion in which many of the poet's belongings have been conserved and exhibited with particular care. Here, too, is the home of Tselementes, and many lovely churches. Both Katavati and Exambela have rooms to rent in both summer and winter.

About a kilometre from Exambela is one of the most historic monasteries on Sifnos, tireless guardian of the island's spiritual and cultural tradition: **the monastery of Panayia tis Vrysis (Our Lady of the Fountain) or Kyra-Vrysiani**. On this site there once stood a church dedicated to the Virgin, around which the wealthy merchant Vasilis Logothetis – a profoundly religious man – constructed a large building complex in 1642. Thus the church was converted into a monastery which played an important role in the life and the society of Sifnos for more than three centuries, and which is still functioning up to the present day. The monastery is arranged in the well-known manner, with the cells and the outbuildings grouped around the katholikon in the centre.

The church is of the cross-in-square type with a dome that rests on an octagonal drum. The exterior supports are octagonal columns. The western bays are covered by cross-vaulting. Outside, the roof consists of a vault that covers the length-wise axis of the church interrupted by a dome on the east. The transept also has a vaulted ceiling. The entrance is on the south side and has a vertical marble border, with brackets and a rectilinear lintel.
There is a second entrance on the west side, surrounded by a similar border. Over the lintel is a semi-circular arched niche.

Inside the church there is a wonderful carved wood templon adorned by some splendid icons. In addition to the templon, there are other remarkable icons which are either hanging on the walls or displayed on icon-stands. Many of these are attributed to the known religious painter Emm. Skordillis. They can be dated to the late 17th or early 18th century, and are fine examples of the so-called Cretan style.

The monastery also houses a **Museum of Ecclesiastical Art and Tradition** in which a large number of artifacts are displayed, such as the handmade prelatic vestment embroidered by Kassiani, the woman who, according to tradition, looked after the little church that existed here in the late 16th century, living as a nun. In order to atone to God for her sin of bringing an illegitimate child into the world, Kassiani embroidered the exquisite vestment that can be seen here. Also on display are manuscript codices, illustrated manuscripts containing the liturgies of Chrysostom, Basil and Pope Gregory of Rome, silver reliquaries, vestments, silver sacred vessels, gospel books, codices, parchments, etc.

1. Katavati.
2, 3. Views from the monastery of Panayia tis Vrysis (Virgin of the Fountain).

Pano Petali, Artemonas

The second largest village on Sifnos is Artemonas. Visitors who want to enjoy the beautiful scenery and the high relief of the Cycladic landscape should not go to Artemonas on the main road that links it with Apollonia, but should instead take the path that starts in Apollonia, goes through the hamlet of **Ano Petali** and ends at Artemonas. The flagstone walk takes you past white houses decorated with Sifnian architectural ornaments, little courtyard fences made colourful by bougainvillaea blossoms, low whitewashed walls and pictures-que churches.

At the highest point of Ano Petali, the visitor will see the **church of Ayios Ioannis**, surrounded by a large churchyard offering a superb view of the surrounding villages.

Half way along the path is the pretty **church of Ayios Antypas**, whose marble lintel bears the date 1636; it also features a chapel built at a later date and dedicated to St Tryphon. The church was rebuilt by the Sifnian priest-monk Nikiforos Troullidis; this was where the first Preparatory School of Sifnos operated in 1821-25.

Wall paintings have been preserved in the sanctuary on the conchs of the prothesis and diakonikon to the right and left respectively of sanctuary apse.

Following the picturesque path, the visitor will arrive at the entrance to Artemonas and see a splendid **church, Panayia "ta Gournia"**, standing to the left. This is the family church of the priest-monk Agapis Procos who has gone down in history by his ecclesastical title Defterevon, with which he signed his paintings that now adorn the church. It is a two-aisled flat-roofed basilica consecrated to the Dormition of the Virgin and to St Nicholas. In its interior, two splendid wooden icon screens have been preserved, together with their exceptional icons, as well as a painted episcopal throne dating from the early 19th century. But the church's wall paintings unquestionably draw the most enthusiastic admiration; they are all excellent works dating from the 19th century. Defterevon, although following the established iconographic programme, did not hestitate to draw from everyday themes and to portray folk tales, legends and symbolic expressions of the period

in unique compositions which he intersperses with his own thoughts and with folk adages. The particular nature of his art will not leave even the most rigorous specialist unmoved. Continuing along the way, you will come to the Nikolaos Chrysoyelos Square, in which the bust of this enlightened teacher stands, and you will see stairs leading up to the village's main square which is dominated by the **church of Ayios Konstantinos**. This is a tile-roofed basilica with three aisles, the only one of its type on the entire island. Inside it, a lovely marble icon screen has been preserved. The icon of the Virgin with Child of the Glykofilousa type is a work of Cretan art, dating probably from the late 16th century, and worthy of note.

Artemonas very likely owes its name to the worship of the goddess Artemis Ecbateria in ancient times. A stroll along its flagstone lanes is an experience which gives the visitor a chance to see some of the most beautiful traditional mansions on the island, set amid lush green gardens. This special little settlement has a kind of magic charm.

Life adjusts to the pace set in the sunny lanes of Sifnos.

The **church of Panayia tis Ammou** (Virgin Mary of the Sand), which is always open, is of particular interest. On the rectilinear lintel of this aisleless flat-roofed church is an incised inscription indicating the date of remodelling as 28 July 1788. Right opposite is the community guest house of Artemonas and a little farther down is the parish **church of Panayia tis Conchis**. This is a three-aisled post-Byzantine church which, according to tradition, took its name from the icon of the Dormition of the Virgin which was found buried in a hollow (conchi) in the road. Opposite the church of Ayios Spyridon is the house in which the great Greek poet Ioannis Gryparis was born; two plaques have been inlaid on its façade testifying to this fact.

At the highest point of the village stand a few traditional windmills; to the left is the **church of Ayia Katerina**, situated on an idyllic site.

Artemonas has a large number of rooms to rent and many visitors prefer to stay here, as it is quieter than Apollonia. In the village you will find the best confectioners' shops and bakeries on the island with traditional Sifnian sweets.

A path to the right off Chrysoyelos Square leads to the **hamlet of Ayios Loukas**, in which is the **church of Ayios Georgios**. Over the cornice at the entrance to the church is a rectangular marble plaque with a carved representation of St George the Dragon Slayer on horseback and dated 1630. On the lovely icon screen inside, there are two significant post-Byzantine icons: one a Deesis (representation of Christ flanked by the Virgin and John the Baptist) a work by Constantinos Palaiokappas dated 1635, and another depicting St George, a work by Zacharias Tzakaropoulos, also dated 1635.

1. The church of Panayia tis Conchis.
2. The home of poet Ioannis Gryparis.
3. Sifnian byways.
4. Artemonas.

On the east side of the island, on top of a precipitous rock with a superb panoramic view of the sea, is the historic village of **Kastro**, undoubtedly the most beautiful part of Sifnos. Life has been going on there independently since the prehistoric period and continues to do so today, defying the passing centuries and retaining some of its old prestige and nobility. On the 3.5 km-long road leading from Apollonia to Kastro, there is a sharp turn at one point in the road, after which the fascinating old village on the rock comes suddenly into view, taking the breath away.

The existence of a settlement on this site from pre-historic times is attested to by the findings of archaeological excavations. The present-day village which was built on the ruins of the ancient capital of Sifnos – which Herodotus called the asty or town – retains to this day the features of a Venetian fortress built during the rule of the Da Corogna dynasty in about 1635. It continues to be one of the most significant settlements with a medieval town plan.

Views of Kastro.

The village was built with respect for the morphology of the terrain, and is purely defensive in nature, as the external walls of the medieval houses form a defensive fortified wall with openings for gates at just five points. Vaulted arcades, or loggias, as they are called, constituted the entrance to and exit from the settlement. During the period of Latin rule, they could be barred shut and every day there was a permanent guard who monitored the traffic in and out of the village. Along the gallery walls we can see the benches that provided rest for travellers and were also used for meetings of the inhabitants when important decisions were about to be made.

The largest and wealthiest houses were in the centre of the village in the inner ring, while the poorer ones were on the outer ring.

All the homes of the notables, as well as the Chancellery, were in the Konakia district in the middle of the village; beside it, on the site known as Despotika, were the residences and offices of the Diocese of Sifnos.

This region was distinguishable in particular for its aristocratic style. In the same district was

The momentary feeling of enclosure created by the loggias and the narrow little streets dissipates in the vastness of the Aegean, visible from most points on the Kastro.

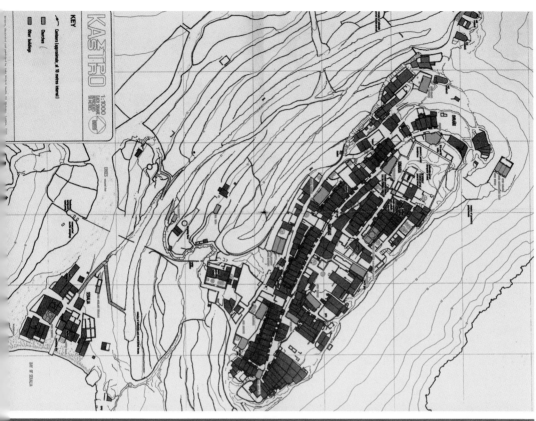

the Roman Catholic cathedral of St Anthony of Padua and a little farther on, the column bearing the inscription of Giannoulis da Corogna from the 14th century.

For security reasons, the main feature of the settlement was its confined space, its lack of public areas, its few little courtyards, its narrow streets which widened out in a few spots, and the single square in front of the church of Ayios Ioannis Theologos (St John the Divine). There was quite a lot of improvisation in the inner layout of the village and many streets were built over the roofs of houses below. The arrangement of the road levels is such that small bridges were frequently built to allow passage. The houses in the Kastro fall into two categories. Those with narrow facades, primarily in the outer ring, were built abutting each other to form the village's continuous outer wall. These are two- and three-storey houses; under this system, horizontal ownership predominates, according to which each floor belongs to a different owner. Access to the upper floors is by exterior stone staircases. On the houses of the outside ring, there are only a few elementary openings outward and no balconies or large windows at all. Such features, wherever they exist, are later additions.

The mansions of the inner ring are distinguished by the existence of a large drawing room around which the bedrooms are usually arranged. This spacious sitting room was unquestionably evidence of the financial well-being of the upper class. In addition, within the residential unit there was a cistern, as well as basins and troughs for feeding livestock. One is impressed by the fact that every bit of space is systematically utilised, even the smallest corner.

Most of the houses on Kastro have relief plaques over the entrance with various symbolic representations and dates. These are the known "family crests", distinguishing features of aristocratic, mainly western European families. Today many of these crests can still be seen on the facades of the houses, untouched by time, to remind the modern visitor of the village's

long, fascinating history.

Walking around the narrow streets of Kastro offers many delights. One might say that in this village, time has stood still, and that a magic breeze blowing gently in the air captivates the visitor, conveying something of the glamour of an age gone by. The narrow stone-paved lanes with their low benches, dark arcades, old homes with little wooden balconies, family crests over the entrances, columns used later as architectural members, marble Roman shrines that are found scattered everywhere with their carved decorations, the loopholes and the tiny courtyards of the houses, but above all the smiling and hospitable inhabitants are part of the unique experience offered by the island, with Kastro as its most pleasant surprise.

In 1930, excavations were conducted on Kastro and in the surrounding area by the British Archaeological School, with significant results. Many of the movable finds from these excavations, as well as various artifacts found in other parts of the island, are today displayed in the **Archaeological Museum** of Kastro, which is located in the inner ring of the village.

The shrines and crests of families that have long since sunk into oblivion can be seen at many points in the picturesque Kastro.

This is a two-storey traditional building, donated by Academician G. Maridakis to the Ministry of Culture. Most of the exhibits can be dated between the end of the 8th century BC and the 3rd and 4th century AD. Here one can see grave stelai, ballot-boxes, a small Cycladic krater and a marble pyx from the 3rd millennium BC, a young man's head and a lion's head from the 6th century BC, a symbolic marble representation of Artemis of Ephesus, a Herm and a Roman head, capitals and a female head from the 4th century BC, and many others. Among the other exhibits in the museum's display cases are shards from Cycladic, Rhodian and Corinthian vessels, mainly from the 7th century BC, terracotta and bronze vessels, ceramic statuettes, among which two female figures from the 7th century BC stand out because of their richly decorated dress, a significant collection of coins which were the bequest of P. Protonotarios, a collection of glass vases from the excavation of the Roman cemetery in the Seralia region, etc.

The visitor can hardly fail to be impressed by the many churches on the Kastro, evidence of the inhabitants' highly developed religious faith. A special place is occupied by the Cathedral, **Panayia Eleoussa**, in the centre of the village. It is an aisleless, domed cross-in-square church. The main entrance is flanked vertically by a marble border, brackets bearing floral decoration, and a lintel on which is a Greek cross and the date 1635 (possibly a renovation date). Over the cornice there is a niche with a perforated plaque bearing a Latin cross surrounded by ships and animals in bas-relief, an indication of the island's seafaring activities. Inside the church, on the north side is a pulpit with a staircase supported on an unfluted column. In the wooden gynaikonitis (part of the church reserved for women), a carved, painted wooden epitaph is kept together with a number of lovely gold embroidered vestments made in Russia and a gold-bound book of gospels printed in Venice in 1862.

On the north wall of the church, in a glass case, is a gold embroidered altar cloth depicting the scene of the lamentation over the death of Christ (Epitaph). On the western wall hangs a debit bond for 500 grossia dated 1814 and signed by Kallinikos Metropolitan of Sifnos. The floor of the church is covered by the marble slabs of six graves. And finally, the church boasts a superb carved wooden icon screen. Of special interest is the icon of the Panayia Vrefokratousa of the Glykofilousa type.

Other important churches in Kastro are the **church of Ayios Nikolaos**, a aisleless flat-roofed church, the **church of Ayia Katerina and Ayios Dimitrios**, a double-aisled church and a flat roof, with an inscription on the lintel dating its renovation to 1653, and an icon of St Demetrius on the templon of the southern aisle, a work by Emmanuel Skordilis dated 1656.

The **church of Ayios Ioannis Theologos** (St John the Divine) on Kastro is an aisleless flat-roofed church with a carved wood templon in good condition. The **church of Ayioi Pantes** (All-Saints) is opposite the Kastro cemetery. The **church of the Kimisis tis Theotokou** (Dormition of the Virgin) is also an aisleless, flat-roofed church; on the marble lintel over the main entrance there is a bas-relief cross within a circle flanked by the date 1593. Inside the church is a splendid marble pulpit and in the sanctuary an altar that rests on a cylindrical marble base adorned with carved representations of rams' heads. The flooring of the church consists of stone slabs and pebble designs. Outstanding among the portable icons is a Panayia Glykofilousa, of the Kardiotissa type, with stylistic elements that date it to the 15th century.

Another significant church is the **Theoskepasti** (Covered by God), an aisleless, flat-roofed structure with pebble floor and carved, painted wood templon on which are icons mainly from the 17th century. The **Christos** (Christ Church) on Kastro is a two-aisled, flat-roofed church with a special orientation. The **Ayioi Saranta** (Forty Martyrs) is a three-aisled, flat-roofed basilica while that of **Ayios Ioannis Prodromos** (St John the Precursor) likewise flat-roofed, but aisleless, also has fine icons on its templon which are in need of conservation. Outside the church of

Ayia Sofia, to the right of the entrance, you can see an inlaid marble plaque on which a female figure in supplication, perhaps the Virgin, has been carved, while an unfluted, gilded column was built into the south wall and visible from outside. On the east side, at the highest point over the apse, another unfluted gilt column has been incorporated.

The Roman Catholic **Church of Ayios Antonis** *(St Anthony)* on Kastro (called Frankantonis), is one of a kind. It is a multi-domed aisleless church built during the period of Venetian rule. The two domes are conic in shape. In the sanctuary there are two altars, the smaller is dedicated to St Anthony of Padua and the larger one to the Abbot St Anthony. The church is not open to the public.

Walking around the outer ring of the Kastro one comes across the ancient wall, while gazing out over the deep blue Aegean. The traveller's gaze will undoubtedly be drawn by the little **chapel of the Efta Martyres** *(Seven Martyrs)* built on a bare rock.

At the foot of the Kastro rock is its little harbour known by the name of **Seralia**. During the period of Latin rule, Seralia was a busy little port handling a fair volume of trade, but today it is virtually uninhabited. Many people come down to the little cove to swim and enjoy the seafood available from the two ouzeries there. They give you a chance to enjoy a meal and watch your cares slip away on the waves of the sea.

1. The chapel of the Epta Martyres or Seven Martyrs.
2. Seralia, the picturesque little port of Kastro.

1

2

Near Seralia is Erkies, a green gully which in antiquity was a cult site of the goat-footed god Pan. Here stands the pretty **church of Ayia Katerina**. To the left, as you leave the village of Kastro, you will see the site on which the famous School of the Holy Sepulchre was established in 1687, which became known as the Public School of the Archipelago. On the site today are two churches, one dedicated to **St John Kalyvitis** and the other to **St Stephen, the first martyr.** The entire walled precinct is the present-day cemetery of the Kastro-dwellers. Opposite, a few traditional mills will see you on your way. The little side road to the right of the road linking Kastro with Apollonia leads to the historic **monastery of Chrysostomos**.

The first recorded accounts of the monastery were found in 1650, which means that it was established at an earlier date. In 1671 the status of the monastery was raised to that of stavropigiki, i.e. it was directly dependent on the Ecumenical Patriarchate, and functioned as such until it was closed in 1834.

After the monastery closed, the building for a while housed the so-called Hellenic school of Sifnos (an old type of school between the elementary and lower secondary level), known by the name Phyteia.

There is a significant incised inscription on a stone in the entrance bearing the date 1653, referring to a pledge that had been given at that time with respect to freeing the country from the Ottoman yoke: this indicates the establishment of the first branch of the revolutionary organisation Philiki Etairia on Sifnos. The main monastery church is a post-Byzantine, domed cross-in-square with a shortened transverse arm. The floor inside the church is marble and includes a slab bearing a double-headed eagle and the date 1818. There is a remarkable painted wooden icon screen with icons dating mainly from the 17th and 18th centuries. The oldest icon on the templon is that of the Panayia inscribed with the name "Amolyntos" (Undefiled), bearing the date 22 July 1659. A visit to this lovely monastery, whose buildings bear witness to the historic memory of the island, can be a moving experience. A characteristic feature of the complex is the stately palmtree standing in the monastery courtyard.

A short road from Artemonas leads to a beautiful bay with steep vertical cliffs that drop straight into the sea. Its official name is **Dialiskari**, but it is better known as Poulati. The **church of Panayia Poulati** is a pristine white jewel in a wild, natural setting. Perhaps the most enjoyable route you could choose is the delightful little path that starts out from Kastro and 20 minutes later comes out into the churchyard. Along the way you will pass the pretty little **chapel of Sotir** with a superb view of the sea.

The church of the Panayia, distant and beautiful, imposes its presence on the surrounding area which is dusty green with olive trees. It is dedicated to the Annunciation of the Virgin and, according to the inscription accompanying the Annunciation scene depicted on the marble plaque over the entranceway, it was established in 1871 and opened in 1875. This is an aisleless domed church of the shortened cross-in-square type, where the transept arms are created within the thickness of the north and south wall.

Our attention will be drawn by the sky-blue dome resting on a high 12-sided drum pierced by four single-light windows, while on the other sides there are closed semicircular niches. All around, on the lower part, there is a horizontal cornice crowned with terracotta acroteria. The church is surrounded by a stone-paved courtyard which contains six cells and the tomb of the Metropolitan Eustathios of Troas (1864-1944) and offers an exceptional view of the sea. The little bay in front of the church attracts many visitors, some of whom enjoy diving off its steep (but dangerous) cliffs; others prefer fishing in its crystal waters.

The road that leads to Herronissos, the northernmost bay on Sifnos, starts out in the main square of Artemonas. The route through the interior of the island gives the visitor an excellent opportunity to become acquainted with the natural environment since there is very little residential development there. Along the way, a side road heading off to the left leads to the

pretty **church of Panayia Mangana**. This is an aisleless domed church that belongs to the shortened cross-in-square type.

Inside the church, the floor consists of plaques and pebbles laid out in geometric, mainly lozenge-shaped designs. In the centre there is a slab bearing a double-headed eagle and the date 1783. South of the church is a stone-paved courtyard with cells to the west and the entrance to the east.

Continuing along the same route, the visitor will encounter the small traditional settlement of Troullaki with its few houses, adorned by the **church of Panayia Troullakiani**. This is a small aisleless church with a dome, of the shortened cross-in-square type. Inside the sanctuary, at an earlier date, there must have been wall paintings under the whitewashed plaster, as can be concluded by the specimen visible on the diakoniko conch (to the left of the main apse).

1. The monastery of Chrysostomos.
2. The monastery of Profitis Ilias (Troullaki).
3. The church of Panayia Poulati.

The road, after Troullaki and up to the harbour of Herronissos, has been paved. **Herronissos** is a lovely fishing village nestled in its little bay, and retaining a charming simplicity. The ouzeri and fish tavernas in the area have been built right on the sandy beach. Any time of the day you may wish to visit this village, you'll be surprised by the calm that prevails. It is not accidental that many of the local people have small houses here that they keep as summer cottages for their holidays. Alongside the beach is a small potter's shop in which one can find attractive handmade ceramic creations including works by Sifnian folk artists.

Herronissos: moments to enjoy graphic Sifnos.

5 SOUTHERN

Monastery of Panayia "to Vouno" - Monastery of Chrysopiyi

Starting from Apollonia, the visitor can explore the island's lovely beaches and enjoy the Sifnian coastline. The second itinerary has been designed for-lovers, with visits to the beaches of Platis Yialos, Vathi and Faros.

SIFNOS

Platis Yialos - Faros - Vathi - Acropolis of Ayios Andreas

The Monasteries of Panayia "to Vouno" (Virgin of the Mountain) and Chrysopiyi (Golden Fountain) and the Acropolis of Ayios Andreas are some of the stops along the way that offer a wide range of interesting sights.

Following the paved road leading from Apollonia to Platis Yialos, you will see a side road leading off to the right which will take you to the **monastery of Panayia "to" Vouno"**, built on a hillside and offering a panoramic view. According to tradition, the construction of the monastery was initiated in 1813 by the monk Gerasimos Avranopoulos, who rescued the icon of the Virgin from the sea and built a church consecrated to her, upon instructions given to him by the Virgin herself in a dream. This icon is known as Panayia Maherousa (date 1756). The monastery is laid out in the usual fashion.

The main church (katholikon) in the centre was built early in the 19th century as an extension to the old church dating from the mid-17th century. In building the new one, Doric columns and capitals from an ancient structure were used.

This is an inscribed cross church with four columns (tetrastyle), and five domes which rest on high drums.

Regarding the church's three aisles, the middle one is dedicated to the Presentation of the Virgin, the left aisle to Sts Constantine and Helena and the right one to St Nicholas. The wall paintings in the right aisle were executed, according to an inscription, by the Sifnian artist Apostolos Sgourdaios. This church was particularly well constructed. It has a carved wood icon screen. In the abbot's quarters of the monastery one can see vestments and ecclesiastical vessels, and for years there has been a large visitor's book to allow people to record their thoughts and good wishes.

To the east of the monastery is a spacious stone-paved courtyard surrounded with benches. Here, especially in summer months, you can see painters, engravers and artists from all corners of the earth, recording the marvellous, devout surroundings in their works. Following the road toward Platis Yialos, another side road leads to one of the

The monastery of Panayia "to Vouno".

most beautiful and famous sites on the island, the holy rock of Chrysopiyi. The view of the little promontory on which the **monastery of Chrysopiyi** stands proudly is positively breathtaking. The split rock with the pristine white building, the sparse vegetation, the vastness of the Aegean and the serene grandeur exuded by the site, all contribute to creating a real visual delight for anyone lucky enough to behold it.

There are countless legends and traditions associated with the building of this monastery, the splitting off of the holy rock connected to the land by a small bridge and the miraculous icon of the Panayia Chrysopiyi (Virgin of the Golden Fountain). The icon depicts the Virgin in her iconographic form as Font of Life, to whom more than 35 miracles are attributed. Tradition tells us that the icon was found floating on the waves by fishermen. Regarding the history and building of the monastery, we can draw considerable information from a manuscript by the priest monk Parthenis Chairetis in the 17th century. The Chrysopiyi has been a dependency of the Monastery of the Panayia tis Vrysis since the mid-18th century. It consists of the church, refectories and cells to the west of the katholikon, which were all built at different stages. The poet Aristomenis Provelengios once lived in one of these cells, as declared by a plaque inlaid in the wall.

The church is a aisleless barrel-vaulted basilica; the side walls inside the church are articulated into semi-circular niches (three on each long side), one of which on the south side has been enlarged and is roofed by independent vaulting. Inside, the floor of the church is paved with marble slabs and in the middle is a bas-relief double-headed eagle bearing the inscription 1818. The carved wood icon screen is worthy of note.

Outside the church, in front of the entrance to the west is a small vaulted vestibule over which is a graceful two-light

The holy rock of Chrysopiyi with the monastery of the same name.

bell tower. The entrance door has a marble border adorned with rosettes and brackets, and over the lintel is a wall painting of the Font of Life in a conch. Over the entrance arch two plaques have been preserved bearing an inscription dated 1757. According to the manuscript of Parthenios Chairetis, a small church pre-existed on this site. In 1675 a larger church was built there. The Panayia Chrysopiyi has been the patron saint of Sifnos since 1964 and the monastery is a religious shrine not only for Sifnians but for the people of the Cyclades as a whole. Today, the stark white monastery of the Virgin standing on the split rock looks like a moored ship preparing to set sail on the seas.

A wealth of legends and tradition surround the Monastery of Panayia Chrysopiyi, one of the most picturesque spots on the island.

To the left of the Chrysopiyi is the picturesque **Apokoftos Bay** with its clear waters. It is suitable for swimming and relaxation, and visitors can enjoy a meal in one of the little seaside tavernas nearby. To the right of the rock is **Saoures**, a pebbled bay perfect for fishing.

The next stop is the busy beach of **Platis Yialos**. The vast beach with its golden sands and crystalline waters has singular pleasures to offer. Visitors can swim, take part in sea sports, and enjoy themselves in many other ways. Along the beach are a number of graphic tavernas, coffee and pastry shops, mezedopolia (traditional tavernas that specialise in ouzo and appetizers), bars and a large number of rooms to let, along with luxury hotels. Platis Yialos offers all comforts to ensure visitors a pleasant vacation. It is the most socially "in" resort on Sifnos and welcomes famous visitors every year. People who are interested in browsing through the many pottery workshops will have an opportunity to see and buy works of Sifnian folk art.

On Sifnos, one can choose the solitude of swimming at the Apokoftos beach (1) or take a walk among the potters' shops in the busy seaside village of Platis Yialos (2-4).

About 100 meters from the beach is a community camping site for those who prefer camping vacations. In the evening the area is buzzing with life and entertainment, although it also offers a good many out-of-the-way places for quiet and reflection. Many visitors choose Platis Yialos as a base of operations for their stay on Sifnos, and take daily trips from there to the rest of the island.

Returning from Platis Yialos on the main road to Apollonia, we turn right at the crossroads toward the pretty seaside hamlet of **Faros**. One can visit it either by taking the main road from Apollonia or, of course, by caique. It is a fishing village with just a few houses, rooms for rent, picturesque ouzeries and a small sandy beach with a calm sea. Alongside Faros, the little coves of Phasolos and Glyfos are perfect for people looking for a peaceful swim.

The cosmopolitan resport of Platis Yialos (1,2) and the pretty little inlet at Faros (3).

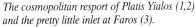

3

Another picturesque bay is the beach of
Vathi. It is about 10 kms of paved road from
Apollonia. This is a small leeward cove with
a pale sandy beach and azure waters lying at
the foot of a verdant green slope. The little inlet
with its calm crystal waters will delight you.
And there is an interesting walk to the nearby
settlement of Vathi which is dominated by the
monastery of the Archangel (Taxiarchis).
Around its two-aisled main church you will find
a dozen or so cells for the accommodation of
visitors. Along the beach there are some
tavernas and restaurants with fresh fish to
satisfy the most demanding diner.

Halfway there, to the right, the visitor can
see the hill of Ayios Andreas with the church
of the same name at the top. The ascent
to the top isn't at all tiring, and takes about
25 minutes on a narrow winding path. The view
from the highest point of the hill is so delightful
that you'll soon forget the effort made to get
there. Here, too, is one of the most significant
archaeological sites on Sifnos: the **acropolis
of Ayios Andreas** which has been preserved in
fairly good condition.

Beside the acropolis stands the **church
of Ayios Andreas** (St Andrew) which, according
to an inscription, was renovated in 1894.
The large stone-paved courtyard all around it
offers the visitor moments of serenity and
contemplation as, from there, they can gaze
out over the sculptured beauty of the Sifnian
landscape all around them. Beside the church
is a structure that belonged to the great
philosopher and theologian Apostolos
Makrakis.

*The church of Ayios Andreas (1)
and the bay at Vathi (2,3).*

2

3

An initial exploration of the region was done by archaeologist Chr. Tsountas in 1898-1899; since then systematic excavations have been conducted by archaeologist Barbara Philippaki, which yielded important information. According to Philippaki, there was very probably a small settlement in this region in the early Cycladic period (3rd millennium BC).

The acropolis is surrounded by a stout double wall. The inner stronger wall was built of Cyclopean masonry and punctuated with eight small rectangular watchtowers, which can be dated chronologically to the period between 1425 and 1100 BC. In a second phase, during the Geometric period (9th-8th century BC), the defences were strengthened by the addition of a crenellated outer wall and a large square tower was built in the northwest corner. The tower divided this area into two unequal parts, making it necessary to construct two small gates in the north and southwest.

The acropolis of Ayios Andreas is 100 x 100 metres in area. Within the citadel enclosure, eight dwellings from the Geometric period have been unearthed. That seems to have been the period of its greatest prosperity. Excavations have brought to light some remarkable finds from the Mycenean, Geometric, Classic and Hellenistic periods.

All of Sifnos is intersected with little paths beckoning travellers to explore. Many such paths around the island lead to one of the countless delightful inlets, serene places for reflection, as well as to more demanding sites for people seeking the adventure of exploration, or who want to get to know every nook and cranny of the island. Many coves are approachable only by the caiques that make the tour of the island, or by private vessels. But whatever you select, one thing is sure: when you leave, the charm of the island is such that it will call you back again and again.

The acropolis of Ayios Andreas.

Bibliography

ALIPRANTIS, C.: Treasures of Sifnos. Icons in churches and monasteries, *Toubi's Editions, 1979.*
"Icons from the katholikon of the Monastery of Ayios Ioannis Chrysostomos Sifnos", *yearbook of the Society of Cycladic Studies.*

DABIS, L. Geological composition of the island of Sifnos, *1966.*

DIMITROKALLIS, G. "Typological and Morphological View of post-Byzantine Church-Building in the Cyclades", Churches in Greece after the Fall of Constantinople, *NTUA, Athens 1993.*

GION, KAROLOS I. History of Sifnos, *Syros 1984.*
History of the Hellenic Nation, *pub. Ekdotiki Athinon.*

KALAMARIS, NIKOLAOS. "Contribution to History by the School of the Holy Sepulchre on Sifnos", *Athens 1960.*

MALLIS, K. – VITSOVITS N. "Sifnos – Cyclades".

PHILIPPA-APOSTOLOU, MARO. "The Kastro on Sifnos", *University of Thessaloniki.*

PHILIPPAKI, BARBARA. "The Prehistoric period on Sifnos", *newspaper Sifnos, No. 149.*
"The Acropolis of Ayios Andreas" *Archaeological Readings from Athens, VI, No. 1 1973.*
"*Sifnos*", Supplement to the Greek edition of the Great Soviet Encyclopedia.

RAMPHOS, IOANNIS SP. (Protopresvyteros) "Deuterevon Sifnos" *(1948)* Kimoliaka C' *(1973).*

SPATHARI-BEGLITI, ELENI. The potters of Sifnos, *1992.*

SYMEONIDIS, SIMOS. History of Sifnos, *1990.*
-- "Monasteries of Sifnos", *(newspaper Kykladiko Fos).*

TROULLOS, ANTONIS. Sifnos, tourist guide, *K. Voutsas Publications.*
Pottery on the island of Sifnos, *1991.*
Sifnos: Marble double-headed and wooden lampstands.
Sifnos: History, Folklore, Tour, *Athens 1974.*
Sifniot Feast, Pilgrim at Panayia Chryssopigi, *1993.*

TZAKOU, ANASTASIA E. Main settlements on Sifnos, *1976.*

VASILIADIS, D. "Flat-roofed post-Byzantine basilicas in the Cyclades",
Introduction to the vernacular architecture of the Aegean Sea, Athens 1955.

VITALIS, PHIL. AP. ARCHIMANDRITE, The Panayia tou Vounou on Sifnos,
publications of the League of Sifnians, 1973

ASHTON, N.G., PANTAZOGLOU, E. Sifnos: Ancient Towers in the Pre-Christian Era. *Athens 1991.*

BROCK, J.K., YOUNG, C.M. Excavations in Siphnos

MILLER, History of Latin Rule in Greece.

ΙΣΤΟΡΙΑ ΤΟΥ ΕΛΛΗΝΙΚΟΥ ΕΘΝΟΥΣ, Εκδοτική Αθηνών.

SW

CO   RT

IN

PEN

3

ROUTES

 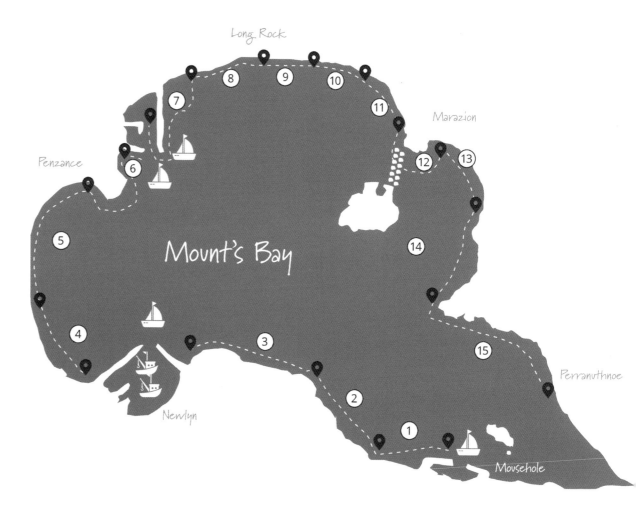

Mount's Bay

Long Rock

Marazion

Penzance

Newlyn

Mousehole

Perranuthnoe

"Not to Scale"

FOREWORD

Note:
Errata
p. 4 ROUTES: For Battery Swim read Green Flag, p.25
For Pier Swim read Red Flag, p.29

I have been swimming the coast of Mount's Bay for 30 years and it is wonderful that Penny and Sand have got together to produce a swimming guide to this extraordinary stretch of coast.

Dedicated to encouraging others to swim in the sea, I have been involved with swim guiding, lifeguard training and open water coaching.

Open water swimming means freedom. It offers adventure and challenges that no indoor pool can replicate.

This little book offers both newcomers to the sport and experienced triathletes a chance to enjoy the coastline of Mount's Bay from the sea. The sense of adventure and achievement is there in every swim - yet every effort has been made to make the reader aware of the conditions and hazards which may be present on each swim.

Of course there is risk, but that assessment has to be made by you, the swimmer. Penny and Sand's wish to promote the sport of open water swimming and the relative safety of this beautiful bay provides the perfect backdrop.

It goes without saying though that every swimmer must expect the unexpected – but at the same time, they can swim without parameters.

Freedom – that's what it is all about. Oh, and cake!

Tina Riggall, RLSS, Lifeguard International

Mount's Bay provides a spectacular introduction to open water swimming and it is astonishingly rich in secret places.
This is the record of our journey.
Penny & Sand

SWIMMING MOUNT'S BAY – THE STORY...

There can be no better way to explore the history and the nature of Mount's Bay (otherwise known as Gwavas Lake) than by taking to the water and swimming the coastline. Although we swim in the Bay on most days of the year, we recognised that we tended to stick to the same sections each time.

So, after a glass of wine in our local, we pledged to expand our swimming horizons and swim Eastwards from Mousehole to Perranuthnoe in a series of short hops between 500m and about 1000m. Whilst we aimed to swim this over the course of 1 hot summer, any part or parts of our journey could also be achieved over a holiday break at any time of year.

We pored over a map in the evenings and walked the coastal path by day searching for suitable entry and exit points. With a little bit of scrambling here and there we had no problem in agreeing our route.

Along the way we researched all the salient features and history of the coastline. We tried out cafés along the way, and where they were sparse we chose suitable stop-off points to enjoy the snacks we had packed so neatly in our swim buoys. At the same time Penny captured scenes in both sketch and oil.

This is an aquatic odyssey to share. So we urge you to take the plunge, release those endorphins and elevate your mood to such a degree that you will want to jump in and swim it all over again – immediately.

Penny & Sand in full gear

Kit & Kaboodle!

Despite the huge fluctuations in sea and air temperature throughout the season we wore the same kit for every swim.

• THE FLEXIBLE TRI SUIT: A wetsuit specifically designed for sea swimming. An ordinary suit will do, and some may be brave enough to don just a cozzie.

• SWIM HAT: The more lurid and luminous, the more we are visible. Also upwards of 30% of body heat is lost through the head. It's a must in the sea.

• GOGGLES: We both prefer the clear goggles to tinted shades.

• EARPLUGS: For those with sensitive cochlear tubes.

• THE HIGH VIZ SWIM BUOY: We have to assume that others cannot see us even if we can see them. The buoys, weightless in water, have another practical function; carrying more kit. We are able to take with us all our own personal belongings, e.g. sandals, car keys, a flask of coffee (for the times there's no nearby café), cake and money for more cake.

OUR JOURNEY

Our journey across the edge of Mount's Bay takes in just under 10 miles of fantastic coastline across this iconic Bay. In a relatively short distance we pass small but bustling fishing villages, a Promenade, working harbours, sandy shores and a remote rugged coastline. There's something for all tastes – and enough adventure for anyone!

We split the route into 4 main sections, each has about 3 different swims, and a bonus section at the end. Of course, you can do these in any order according to where you are, where you want to be – and maybe which café(s) you fancy en route. We work on the basis that for those without a car, starting point is Penzance bus station. Bus info at www.firstgroup.com. Each swim identifies an entry and exit point - you must make an assessment of the best points of access for yourself and your ability. We cannot guarantee any changes to conditions, including tide, weather, etc. and all distances are approximate.

MOUSEHOLE TO NEWLYN We start West and head East. Splitting this phase into 2 or 3 easy swims of about 500m.

NEWLYN TO PENZANCE The most 'urban' swims can be found in this section – and the most abundant section of cafés. Again, 3 swims of about 500/750m.

PENZANCE TO MARAZION Swims across the beautiful Long Rock and Marazion beaches. 6 swims in all along this route - although stronger swimmers will do this in about 3 or 4 swims. (This section includes a magical swim across the St Michael's Mount causeway – one of our favourites).

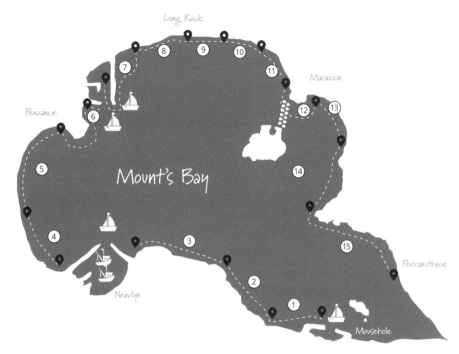

Total distance - 8.5 miles/13.7k
Walking time (via South West Coastal Path) - 3 hours

MARAZION TO PERRANUTHNOE The most isolated swims heading out across the rugged coastline to Perranuthnoe. 1 easy swim and 2 bigger ones (about 1,000m) due to limited accessibility.

THE BONUS SWIMS Some interesting 'off piste' swims to and around iconic islands.

We try to add some interesting facts along the way - sometimes history, geography or the environment. We also make sure we talk about the cafés (and cake) we find on each section. This is about the pleasures of the journey. We share our experiences with you – sometimes written with an individual voice or together. No swim is ever the same – the conditions, the things that happen on the way – and that's what makes sea swimming such a joy. We hope you enjoy creating your own adventure.

SWIMMING IN THE SEA

A word on safety.... If in doubt – get out!

Not every swim we attempted worked out. Conditions ruled our decision-making. Sometimes we never even dipped our toes. Other times we cut short our planned distance and headed for the shore which is why we scan our route for quick exits. Someone always knew where we were going and when we were due back - and often we'd have 'watchers' on shore walking the coastal path.

We have tried to give an indication of the overall level of ease and safety based on our ability as moderately good open water swimmers who can freestyle. Every day is different, so you must give each swim your own honest assessment. If you feel at all uncomfortable or unsafe, exit the water. We did, more than once. We use the following 'flags' as an indication – all swims are relatively easy, but conditions (e.g. limited 'escape routes', significant water traffic or length) might increase the indicator level :

 "This is just lovely – let me in!"

 "It's OK – I've got a few butterflies though"

 "I'm going to need all those extra laps of training I put in at the pool"

TIDES & TEMP

High water, low water, spring tide, neap tide, slack water, swell, rip...

The sea has a vocabulary of its own and we soon learned that our journeys were best taken within 2 hours of high tide and in the more unknown territory we swum at slack water. This is the period where the tide barely moves so we were less exposed to the vagaries of strong currents. Homework on the area and knowledge of tides are an essential prerequisite to each swim.

The sea temperature was at its lowest in the spring when we first embarked on our project. At a little over 10 degrees Centigrade; (absolutely breath-removing cold) we selected short stretches with multiple exit points. As the season progressed, our confidence soared with the temperature and by July we were swimming in a whopping 17 degrees.

So we picked our places according to wind and weather.
We never swam alone and we learned to expect the unexpected.

CAKE AND ART EN ROUTE

This book is about swimming, but we also wanted our journey to be a pleasurable 'whole' experience beyond the swims themselves.

So as well as the gorgeous West Cornwall scenery and the sea, we've added 2 other ingredients – art and cake.

Penny is a well-known Cornwall-based artist, and brings a unique perspective to her images of seascapes – often from within the sea itself. We hope the images of the journey also inspire you to experience them for real.

We really like a good coffee and cake! So we made sure we tried out lots of cafés en route. We don't intend this to be a 'Trip Advisor' set of recommendations, so it's pot luck whether you get good service and cake – although we say as we find here. Each section gives the reader a starter for 10 on local cafés, but our list is not exhaustive.

Given the nature of our route, there are sections with no choice at all. In these instances we became adept at packing a thermos flask and cake into our safety buoys. Not sure that was ever the purpose for which they were designed – but it worked for us.

After a swim, we would change and head to a café. Some other times (when it was a trek back to the car) we'd stay in our (wet) wetsuits, and we would often shout our order through the door so as not to leave puddles – and usually the staff were kind and brought out our coffee and cake. In the summer months there are several mobile cafés along the way, which makes life much easier when you're wet.

We also varied our treats with ice cream when it was especially hot.

One little tip, it's easy to forget when you're swimming distances and see so much water around you, that you can become de-hydrated, especially swimming in hot sun. Drink plenty of water, as well as coffee and cake. We put a squeeze of lemon juice in ours which helps get rid of the salty after-taste of sea water. No matter how hard we try, we always end up with 'sea mouths'!

We wanted this set of swims to be a pleasurable way to experience our lovely home in West Cornwall. The swims and the scenery will be enough for some. For others, the cake will add to the adventure.

MOUSEHOLE
TO NEWLYN

SOLOMON BROWNE

On 19th December 1981 the lifeboat Solomon Browne, based at the old Penlee Lifeboat Station, was called out to aid the vessel Union Star, a cargo vessel on its maiden voyage. On board the Union Star was the crew of 5, the Captain's wife and his 2 daughters.

Caught in heavy gales, the vessel's engines failed and a 'mayday' call was sent out.
Captain Trevelyan Richards and his crew of 7 set off at once to the Station.

The Mousehole men managed to rescue 4 of the passengers in a huge sea, and Captain Richards then radioed ashore to say that the lifeboat was going in again to try and save the remaining 4.

That's when disaster struck.

The presumption is that a huge wave dashed the boats together and both then sank. Everyone, including the entire crew of the Solomon Browne, perished.

Today the lifeboat station, with its steep slip and red doors, stands as a permanent memorial to the 8 brave men who died trying to save the lives of others.

1. PENLEE SWIM

Parking:
Mousehole Car Park (£)
or along the road (free).

Bus:
M6 from Penzance

Entry/Exit points:
Mousehole Harbour/steps from road
down to Skilly Beach.

Length of swim:
750m

Conditions for our swim:
Northerly wind, outgoing tide, slightly
choppy water.

Today we plan to swim through the harbour mouth and out into the ocean towards Penlee Point. Boats on their moorings crowd the inner harbour and children paddle happily in the shallows. But the moment we pass through the gap the sea pounces on us and we bob about in an angry swell. White horses bicker at the rocks. The sun beams down upon us and although the azure blue is most alluring our relationship with the water is not going well. The sea didn't seem quite this bouncy when we viewed it from the shore.

"Sand," I yell across the divide. "We're swimming against the wind and tide. Why make it hard for ourselves? Let's swim this leg in reverse."

A swift thumbs up confirms her agreement and we head for the shore immediately. To stay warm we jog along the coastal path towards Penlee Point. Access to the point is about half a mile further East and after going right down the access path opposite the flat roof houses, we are strolling happily along a concrete promenade. This is Skilly Beach and we're heading for the old lifeboat house. Just as the path peters out we locate a natural pier of flat rocks and prepare to swim West around the point.

The sea sucks and blows and we choose our moment to slither into the ocean.

We're in! Again.

I float a little and feel the push of the wind which has suddenly become our friend as it nudges us towards Mousehole. The surface explodes with the glitter of sunshine. I glance to my left and take in St Michael's Mount, the talisman that will be in our sights on every leg of our swim.

It takes us almost 10 minutes to round Penlee Point and pass the red doors of the old lifeboat station.

I glance out into the Bay and spot the big marker buoy known as Low Lee. There are wrecks on the reef below and divers frequent the area in search of a lost past. The water is deep here and for a moment I think about the other world 40 feet down. A sea bed with a life of its own and with a history covered with sand and debris.

The water calms and we are in our stride – or should I say stroke. I call for a puff break and as we tread water and take stock, a seal catches our eye. His big be-whiskered face angles this way and that.

Is he winking? This is his element and we know he is tailing us as every now and then a dark shadow flashes past.

And now we are approaching the harbour wall. No more need for puff breaks. We gather speed as we near our destination. Looking ahead I notice we have an audience. Tourists chatter and point as we enter the harbour. A young mum steps forward from a group. "I've got to ask – why have you got those orange things round your waist?" Sand and I look bemused. Oh, we work for the post office. On a busy day it's quicker to swim the mail round to Mousehole than drive from Newlyn. No – that's too close to the truth. Sand shrugs and plumps for truth. "So everyone can see us coming…" and, given the little audience we had that day – they certainly did!

Cake stop!

We are spoilt for choice in Mousehole.

Jesse's dairy (11 Fore St) sells amazing ice creams – and does an excellent cream tea.

There are plenty of others in this lovely old fishing village (The Old Pilchard Press, Four Teas, Rock Pool).

We chose a take away coffee and a flapjack (delicious) from the wonderful 'Hole Foods' Deli which is situated right on the harbour front (North Cliff Rd).

You can sit down and eat inside, or like us, stand outside dripping wet and shout your order through to the very kind and helpful staff. We sat on the conveniently placed stone seats looking out over the harbour. Heaven!

2. SKILLY BEACH SWIM

Parking:
Roadside (free).

Bus:
M6 from Penzance

Entry/Exit points:
Skilly Beach

Length of swim:
300m

Conditions for our swim:
Slack tide. High visibility. Flat calm.
In other words, just lovely!

Locals love this bay. As we clamber down and once again saunter towards the lifeboat house we see fisherman spinning for their supper. Idlers skim stones while their partners snooze on this languorous Sunday afternoon. We re-trace our steps but today all is calm and the sea whispers encouragement. This gently sloping beach – a mixture of grey sand and shingle - is truly tranquil.

The water is translucent and we swim slowly taking in the flora and fauna below and the panoramic vista above. There are marker buoys left by the boatmen seeking crabs and lobsters. This is good ground for crustaceans but the abundance of life is not always desirable. In late summer, the prevailing Southwesterly currents bring in a spectacular array of jellyfish. A wetsuit gives us good protection and we have a little knowledge regarding these unwelcome creatures. We have read that shaving soap soothes a sting. A credit card scraped across the skin draws out the poisonous tentacles. Vinegar is an excellent antidote to the pain. Is there no end to the paraphernalia we cram into our buoys?

We use the flat topped houses on the road above the bay as a marker while swimming and head inland. Then as we sip hot coffee from our flasks Sand suggests a little more jellyfish research to ease our minds.

Cake stop!

We brought our own for this one - although if you fancy a short walk (10 mins) you can head back into Mousehole for the selection of cafés listed on the Penlee Swim.
Perhaps changing first...

FRIENDS IN THE WATER?

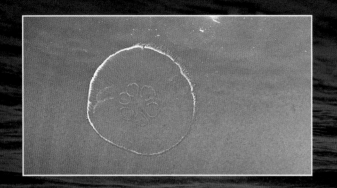

First up is the moon jellyfish (Aurelia aurita), one of our most common jellies. They float near the surface with the current and are virtually transparent bar their rose-coloured gonads in the centre which are shaped like circular petals. Their stinging power is not enough to penetrate the skin and one may feel a slight irritation, but we have found them to be totally harmless and have never felt a thing when handling them.

Now the blue jellyfish (Cyanea lamarckii) is not quite so touchable. It has a blue/purple tone and long tentacles. In British waters it is quite small –10-20cm. Their attack can feel like a nettle sting or to some, like a wasp sting.

The compass jellyfish (Chysaora hysosella) has 16 dark 'V' shaped lines radiating from the centre and dark points all around its circumference. Apparently the sting feels like a small electric shock. It is easily recognisable in the water and is also very lovely. These jellies tend to drift along below the swimmer so contact is not common. As an avoidance tactic I suck in my breath and, like a startled bird, make myself thin as an arrow, so as to glide safely across the surface leaving this graceful jelly to potter along at its own pace.

Once, when swimming across Sennen Beach, I was all of a quiver as first my feet and then my hands came into contact with hard, rubbery slime.

It was a plague of moon jellies but as I tore out of the water in horror, a child of around 5 halted me and handed over an example of the slithery enemy that was Aurelia aurita.

"They don't hurt," she said. "Look at it. Isn't it very lovely?"

NEWLYN TIDAL OBSERVATORY

Look up at the lighthouse. The small unassuming building next to it is the Newlyn Tidal Observatory which houses a simple domed brass bolt set in a recess in the floor.

The top of this bolt is the bench mark for all tidal height measurements in the whole of Great Britain.

The site was selected as it is here that the Atlantic ocean is most reliable compared with other parts of the coast.

So what?

Well the observatory was set up in 1915 which means that for over 100 years data has been contributing to studies in oceanography, geology and in particular, climate change.

So not only are all tide timetables based on the Newlyn tides but every variation in sea level is monitored and detailed.

3. SANDY COVE SWIM

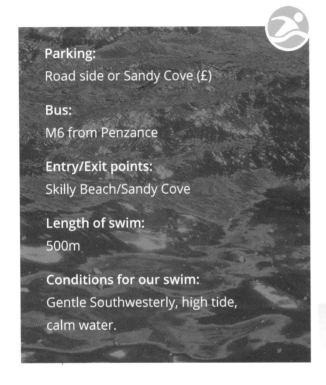

Parking:
Road side or Sandy Cove (£)

Bus:
M6 from Penzance

Entry/Exit points:
Skilly Beach/Sandy Cove

Length of swim:
500m

Conditions for our swim:
Gentle Southwesterly, high tide, calm water.

For the third and final time on this section, Penny and I access the sea via the steep track down to Skilly Beach.

We enter the sea immediately to the left at the bottom of the first access point to the water. There's a conveniently placed narrow channel heading South. It's a fantastic way to enter the water – there's almost an invisible pull which takes you gently through the channel and out into the open water.

There is a lot to take in and even at high tide the water is shallow here with great underwater rock pools. We hug the coast, past hidden tunnels that provided access to the old Penlee quarry. In its heyday thousands of tons of granite were blasted out and transported to the rest of the country by sea.

On a calm day the metal ruins of the old rail workings are visible so keep an eye out for any sharp objects close to the surface. We head towards the first pier. With the wind directly behind us we whizz along. The first pier rears up in no time – Swordfish Pier – a favourite haunt for fishermen, so watch out for their lines. The pier commemorates the biplane named Swordfish which was operated by the Royal Navy throughout the 2nd World War.

Cake stop!

In the interests of research (!) we changed and headed back to Mousehole for coffee & cake.

Newlyn is just as close (see café list in Tolcarne Swim). We went to try out the Rock Pool café.

Not the cheapest, but really excellent coffee and cake.

It's a popular spot so be warned - you might not get a seat. If weather permits try to sit outside in the pretty courtyard overlooking St Clement's Isle - we swim around this in our bonus swims.

We ease into Sandy Cove which, due to the activities of the quarry, is no longer sandy. However, it is a quiet and sheltered beach. The 2nd pier – South Pier, marks the perimeter edge of the harbour and when the Easterly blows strong, an enormous wave is created that barrels up against the pier and is referred to by surfers as the Boneyard, as this beach and area was once a place where old boats were set alight and destroyed.

WARNING

Don't swim too close to the pier as not only is Newlyn Harbour one of the busiest fishing ports in the country but also there is an unpleasant rip which can hold you right up against the wall.
We wouldn't recommend going round the harbour wall from Sandy Cove.
Clamber out on the beach instead – it's a bit pebbly so mind your toes!

NEWLYN TO
PENZANCE

NEWLYN HARBOUR

Newlyn is an important fishing port, it has one of the highest values of landings in the entire country – some £28 million per year. The fleet is composed mainly of 'Beam Trawlers' which can spend several days at a time at sea. There are also many ring netters working the Bay for sardines (pilchards), mackerel and more recently anchovies. Alongside these are crabbers and hand-liners – types of boats which have been fishing from Newlyn for centuries.

4. THE TOLCARNE SWIM

Parking:
Tolcarne Car Park (£)

Bus:
M6 from Penzance
(or 30 min walk from station).

Entry/Exit points:
Steps by fisherman's statue/
Wherrytown slip

Length of swim:
500m

Conditions for our swim:
We swam early in the season, no wind, flat calm, temp was just above 10 degrees. Gentle Southwesterly.

We meet at the steps next to the life-sized bronze statue of a young fisherman casting his line.
The statue by Tom Leaper was made in memory of all fishermen who died at sea. Unveiled in 2007, this magnificent sculpture is a stirring and poignant reminder of the dangers of the sea.

In years past there was an annual swim from this statue, along the Prom and all the way to the Jubilee Pool, a distance of 1450 metres. This popular event was known as the Yacht swim as a pint in the pub of that name after the race was essential. The race was attended by upwards of 500 swimmers of all ages and standards and the winners achieved the distance in around 16 minutes. A truly Olympian speed.

Today with temperatures at only 10 degrees we don't plan to be in the water longer than 16 minutes and swim furiously towards the first slip, heading East along the promenade. The sea is calm and clear. A gentle Southwesterly helps us on our way. We cross Lariggan Rocks, the reef off Wherrytown and splash to the slip. There's history in the smooth granite slabs. They were laid for a quay built in the 19th Century to receive serpentine from the Lizard and minerals from Wheal Wherry, the tin mine built right out at sea opposite the quay. Visited by Prince Albert in 1848, the slip was home to the first Penzance /Newlyn Lifeboat. As we run back to our start point, I regale Sand with this information – it's a good way of stopping my teeth from chattering.

She's not listening. Her thought is of hot tea and cake and our destination is the Duke Street Café.

Cake stop!

Lots of great little café stops in Newlyn – although we'd suggest you get changed first (it's a busy working fishing village and wetsuits probably aren't the best here).

We went to the really great Duke St café (Duke St Car Park). There's good coffee and fantastic cakes at Warren's (opposite Duke St).

Other places to try include the Newlyn Filmhouse (5 mins walk from the centre up The Coombe) or the café in the Newlyn Art Gallery which has amazing views from a picture window overlooking the bay.

5. PROMENADE SWIM

Parking:
Boating Lake (free)/St Anthony's Car Park opposite Jubilee Pool (£)
Promenade (free)

Bus:
10–20 min walk from station depending on start point.

Entry/Exit points:
Slip near to Yacht Pub on Promenade/ End of Prom or Wherrytown slip

Length of swim:
1000m

Conditions for our swim:
Strong Easterly, incoming tide. Temp around 12 degrees.

There's a strong Easterly blowing so Penny and I make the executive decision to achieve this swim in reverse – starting at Jubilee Pool slipway and heading West towards Newlyn. With the sea still slow to warm up, this was an excellent idea and we skate along the surface at great speed.

Approaching the Queen's Hotel, the sea bounces off the Prom wall creating unusual undulations. The two parallel roads running either side of the Hotel often cause strange but essentially weak eddies. We're prepared for this bounce. There's no point in fighting it and we bob along like a pair of corks.

With a watcher promenading alongside us and many exit points via steps, this is a perfect spot for a serious swim with plenty of 'bail out' stops.

On an incoming tide it's easy to get pulled into the prom wall, so watch out for this. If the sea is clear there are interesting changes between sand and rock – and it's surprising how often you'll see a shoal of little darting fish. Watch out for a regular seal on this route, they seem to like the company on this busy stretch. You'll also see a lot of fellow swimmers here – some of whom will stop to chat. And suddenly it's done. Penny and I float on our backs for a while revelling in the movement of the sea. We exit the water and head for the mobile café on the Prom.

Cake stop!

We're spoilt for choice in Penzance for excellent places to eat. This end of town has a few to choose from including Zebra Crossings (Morrab Rd) and the Little Wonder Café (parked in the promenade gardens).

For this swim, we chose to stay in our wetsuits and sat in a couple of deckchairs outside the mobile café called the TinBox Coffee Co.

The coffee here really set the highest standard for anywhere we stopped – and the cakes weren't bad either. The lovely man serving us wanted to know all about what we were up to – I don't suppose there were many customers that day dressed from head to toe in rubber?!

6. BATTERY SWIM

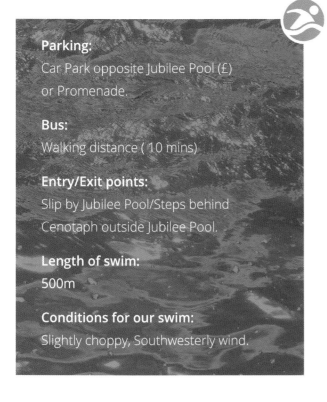

Parking:
Car Park opposite Jubilee Pool (£)
or Promenade.

Bus:
Walking distance (10 mins)

Entry/Exit points:
Slip by Jubilee Pool/Steps behind
Cenotaph outside Jubilee Pool.

Length of swim:
500m

Conditions for our swim:
Slightly choppy, Southwesterly wind.

Starting from the slip we swim around the perimeter of the iconic Jubilee Pool. A masterpiece of art deco architecture, the lido suffered terrible damage in the storms of 2014 and had to be rebuilt. It is a hub of family fun in the summer and will boast a geothermal pool – a necessary hot tub after larking around in freezing water. We discover our swimming speed as we watch the letters of JUBILEE POOL slip past. At approximately 7 seconds per letter we are delighted and hope to keep up the pace for the entire duration.

Ahead is the promontory named Battery Rocks where there was a gun battery to repel the French. There is a plaque laid by Queen Victoria at the tip of the railings down into the sea, as this has been a popular sea swimming spot since the 1880's. Looking out towards the horizon, there is the tall red and black striped Gear Pole which marks the end of a long reef. According to one internet observation, prehistoric tools made from rock on this reef were found in Scotland. Now how would one prove that without spending too much money?

Today there must be a few currents running around Battery Rocks as the temperature drops dramatically when we round the corner. Fortunately the tidal flow carries us speedily into calm waters on the leeward side. There's an abundance of different seaweeds; bladderwrack, laminaria, sea thongs and coralline weed. In amongst the weed are spider crabs, starfish and wrasse. To our right is the large raised rock called Carn Olven, a favourite spot for seals and cormorants. We continue along the harbour wall. Yachts are anchored outside the harbour on free moorings and the beautiful black and white lighthouse rears up. We tread water and take in our surroundings before turning and heading back to the Cenotaph where we clamber along the rocks and up the concrete steps.

Cake stop!

We try out the café in Jubilee Pool - you can access this without paying for entry to the Pool, although we recommend you try out the pool too (maybe on a rest day from swimming the Bay!) A reasonable coffee and cake - there's a bit of a wait if it's busy.

PICKING UP
AN ENTOURAGE

We often have an entourage with us when we're out swimming. Swans live happily on the water near the stream outlet at Wherrytown and they glide alongside us in a graceful manner as we slog it out across the Prom. Powerful and sometimes aggressive, swans have a reputation for attacking innocent bystanders but so far, we have never been threatened by these residents even when they have their cygnets in tow. This particular family seem to enjoy the shores of Penzance as much as we do and are well-loved by the locals.

Seals too, accompany us along our route. St Clement's Isle is home to several mothers and pups. Lone bachelors come inland for a nose around, especially near the harbour where there may be an ample food source from returning fishing vessels. Below us, behind us or ahead, these seals make great companions. Their soft brown eyes and long whiskers

give them a playful appearance and again, we have never given them any cause to display their strength. We don't linger with them – the ocean is vast and there is space for all.

In June, spider crabs wave their long claws and starfish gather amongst the rocks. Flatfish such as plaice and megrim stir up the sand below and pollock hover nervously amongst the seaweed. Dolphins may leap and laugh in the distance but we have yet to pick up any Cetacean companion.

Both herring and black backed gulls breed on the cliff and rocky outcrops. They will dive-bomb the hapless swimmer if they are protecting young. We appreciate their dilemma and keep a good distance from their nesting spots.

One visiting swimmer at Battery Rocks showed me a 2-inch white scar on the back of his hand. "Beware the gannet," he said. "My little fingers looked like

small fry in the water as I swam in my black wetsuit. Swimming freestyle, I never even saw the gannet take his dive, but I certainly felt his beak when it penetrated my hand." He must have been a long way out to sea when that happened. I know that death by gannet was a medieval punishment meted out in Scotland.

How? Well, OK I'll tell you. The helpless victim was chained and submerged in the sea leaving only his head above water. Bait was placed on the victim's head and when the gannets spotted their lunch they dived. This is trepanning of the most awful kind.

PENZANCE TO
MARAZION

7. PIER SWIM

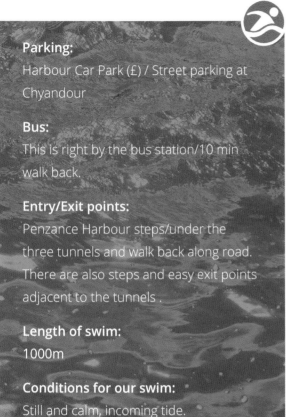

Parking:
Harbour Car Park (£) / Street parking at Chyandour

Bus:
This is right by the bus station/10 min walk back.

Entry/Exit points:
Penzance Harbour steps/under the three tunnels and walk back along road. There are also steps and easy exit points adjacent to the tunnels .

Length of swim:
1000m

Conditions for our swim:
Still and calm, incoming tide.

We park in the harbour car park and make our way to the end of Albert Pier. The tide is high and there is plenty of activity in the harbour.

During the winter, the harbour and the Abbey Pool on the other side of Ross Bridge are both excellent places for a safe if freezing dip. Nothing makes the adrenaline surge faster than a plunge into water below 10 degrees. The boats over-winter on dry land so swimmers can frolic safely. This is also a good point to practice swimming in the sea and acclimatise if you haven't done it for a while. Watch out for kids jumping in off the Ross Bridge over your head though!

On the day of our swim, children are leaping in from the end of the pier squealing with fear and delight. Sand and I make a more elegant entry down the steps and glide gently round the end of the pier. I wonder where the children thought we were going as we headed off out of the harbour – but didn't return?

Conditions are perfect – they need to be as there are no exit points along the length of the pier.

Sometimes our minds can begin an unhelpful monologue of pessimistic backchat. I know Sand hated this bit.

"Bad voice: There's no way out along this pier.

Good voice: But it's only 200m long.

Bad voice: What if you get cramp?

Good voice: Shut up and concentrate on your stroke."

I try to think of something to calm me...

Jenny, my swim coach, gave me some useful tips regarding my arm stroke last February.

"It's all about visual thinking," she said. "First, attach a paintbrush to your elbow and paint the sky as you lift it from the water. Secondly, lead with your hand and let that arm pierce the water like a javelin. Finally, stretch out for your gin and tonic and scrape your hand down to the sand below."

I begin a rhythmic mental chant. Paintbrush, elbow, sky, arm, javelin, gin.

Scrape sand, spill gin, paint sky again. Paint brush..... And so the time passes speedily, my stroke improves and I can now spot exit points all along the rocks.

We swim in a more leisurely fashion around the perimeter of the rocks passing the railway station and groups of fishermen. We're heading for the three tunnels, a place where tin, mined in St Just, was shunted by rail and loaded onto ships. The mines, owned by the Bolitho estate are now derelict, but the estate office (once the Bolitho Bank) still functions as the business hub. Visible from the pier, we lose sight of the tunnels as we hug the coastline. We know when we've almost reached our destination as the water chills noticeably. A fresh stream dashes through the tunnels and we raise our pace to keep warm. Two of the arched tunnels are full of seawater.

We elect not play at extreme pot-holing and instead clamber through the third tunnel and over the pebbles as the tide rushes in, scoops us up and we are deposited onto the high water line. It's a good distance and we pat ourselves on the back as we plod back past the station and onto the harbour for tea and cake.

Sand gave this a 'red' swim as she felt the same about lack of easy exit points.

Cake stop!

This end of Penzance is full of great cafés - everything from a traditional 'greasy spoon' (the anything but greasy Sullivans Diner on the corner of the bus station which does amazing bacon butties - OK, not cake, but sometimes after a swim it's hard to beat) to a great deli/café (try Helly's on the front/Wharf Rd which also has discounted coffee before 10am) and cosy little cafés such as the Front Room (83 Market Jew St).

A favourite of Sand's is the Portuguese café María Chica (24 Markey Jew St) - mainly because she has a thing about Pastel De Nata!

If you're swimming by the Ross Bridge end, try out Harbour Side Café or the Old LifeBoat.

We really are spoilt for choice here.

8

8. THREE TUNNELS SWIM

Parking:
Street parking at Chyandour.

Bus:
10 min walk from station/10 min walk back (along the road not coastal path).

Entry/Exit points:
Through the tunnels/beach.

Length of swim:
350m

Conditions for our swim:
Northerly wind, outgoing tide, slightly choppy water.

We cross the road to the little patch of shingle by the tunnels. We pick our way gingerly across the stones.

If there's an ominous rumbling whilst you are in the tunnels, it's not the imminent collapse of the bridge, just the train passing through to the station at Penzance.

The sea undulates and bounces around the rocks and we dive into the water. That first plunge is always a wonderful moment. The flow of the tide is with us and we fly past the rocky edge. There's a second tunnel with more freezing water gushing into the sea. We tread water and laugh with delight. The coast here is industrial. Cars flash past on the dual carriageway and I look seawards. Underneath lies an ancient forest and at extreme low tide I can walk among the petrified stumps of oak and pine, the forest where rare and ancient marine creatures live and breed. The dark, hard oak wood is like rock but easily distinguishable. Acorns and cobnuts are washed up with the tide and sometimes great black trunks come rolling up the shore. A sharp reminder that four thousand years ago the Mount was part of the mainland.

We head for the slip near the bridge and have to cross the wooden bridge instead of taking the coastal path back. We look incongruous striding along the main road in our wetsuits and clutching our buoys. A fine swim of a good length yet taking no time at all.

Cake stop!

We brought our own for this one - although if you fancy a short walk (5 mins) you can head back into Penzance for the selection of cafés listed on the Pier Swim. We recommend changing first...

THE FEEL GOOD FACTOR

It goes without saying that swimming in open water has enormous health benefits both physically and mentally. In recent times much research has been undertaken as to precisely what those benefits are and there is an enormous amount of information available both online and in print. So what actually happens when we take the plunge? We're not scientists, but we know we like it – or at least we do afterwards!

So, feeling a bit scientific one day, we attempted to monitor our feelings on a cold, wet November morning and write them down for this book.

We look down into the water with nervous anticipation. We know the temperature is about 12 degrees. Cold enough to really shock our bodies but we're prepared for this. We've done it before and we're getting a little more used to those painful opening seconds... And we're in!

The cold takes our breath away – we're close to the pain barrier – in fact the stress response in our bodies right now is the same as in an animal attack or when sitting a dreaded exam. The fight or flight reaction has kicked in. Our heart rate increases, our blood pressure rises and there's a tiny bit of

panic there too. We swim furiously, arms pumping, breathless and cold to the point of pain. Our faces and hands ache, icy water seeps down the back of our wetsuits in breathtaking rivulets. But the shock brings mental clarity.

We read later that, to help us cope with this initial stress, our parasympathetic nervous system is kicking in and is stimulating the release of endorphins. As our bodies acclimatise to the temperature our muscles relax, our breathing slows along with our heart rate. And this is the moment we have been waiting for. It is why we swim. A kind of meditative peace takes over and we can use our bodies efficiently to slice through the water.

We emerge from the swim giggling like school girls. Our bodies are bright red. We're not sure why or how – but we know we feel much, much better . Ready even to cope with the stresses of daily life and call it a breeze. So what else happened to our bodies while we swam? Well obviously the blood has rushed everywhere, that's why we are so red. So yes, our cardiovascular systems are working pretty well and we could perhaps improve circulation with more swimming to force the heart to work harder.

The cold water has also caused our lymph nodes to contract forcing the system to pump lymph fluids around our bodies which triggers the release of white blood cells to destroy unwanted substances. The claim is now being made that cold water immersion improves the immune system - and certainly more sports men and women use ice water treatments.

Those magical endorphins also inhibit the communication of pain signals and along with the anti-inflammatory effect of cold water on sore muscles, many swimmers report that they feel less pain.

Patients with clinical depression often have low levels of serotonin and dopamine. If open water swimming stimulates the release of these neurotransmitters, then this has to be a great reason why we would want to keep taking that plunge. We just feel good.

Post swim euphoria is not a myth so as we race to the café for cake and coffee we let all our neurotransmitters know that we will definitely do this again.

9. RAILWAY BRIDGE SWIM

Parking:
Long Rock Car Park (£).

Bus:
U4 from Penzance.

Entry/Exit points:
Beach entry /exit.

Length of swim:
400m

Conditions for our swim:
Sunny day, but strong Easterly wind.
Incoming tide.

With a strong Southeasterly blowing we opt for the reverse direction and enter by the car park at Long Rock.

There being no convenient coffee spot on this stretch (we didn't fancy the supermarket), Sand carries a flask of hot coffee in her buoy. I have bananas, my car key and cake. We have to keep an eye out for the kite surfers who are revelling

in the conditions. We pass the big green railway shed in no time – the currents as well as the wind seem to be with us. Yet when we round a bend the beach changes to rock and suddenly the tide is against us. It's safe enough as the water is shallow but after a 100 strokes I have progressed only 50 metres. We shriek with delight as the waves dip and crash around us. When we reach our destination at the railway bridge we clamber up the rocks and Sand unscrews the cap off her Thermos. It's a spring tide but we're well protected and let the spray and surf surround us.

We take the coastal path back to the car park passing numerous runners who are competing in the 32 mile Lizard to Land's End race. They look exhausted. I want to advise them that swimming sedately is a much more genteel occupation. But these guys are competing against themselves in a test of endurance. We smile encouragement and wish them well.

This is an interesting beach at low tide. One day we must return to search out the ancient forest and hunt for the wreck of the French schooner Jeune Hortense which foundered on Long Rock in 1888.

Cake stop!

We brought our own for this one – although if you fancy a short walk (10 mins) you can head across the road bridge into Sainsbury's café – it's OK... We recommend getting changed first.

10. LONG ROCK SWIM

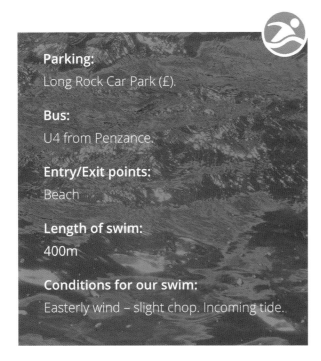

Parking:
Long Rock Car Park (£).

Bus:
U4 from Penzance.

Entry/Exit points:
Beach

Length of swim:
400m

Conditions for our swim:
Easterly wind – slight chop. Incoming tide.

Cake stop!

We brought our own again for this one - although a short walk (10 mins) will take you towards Marazion for a selection of cafés (see Paddleboard and Causeway Swims).

It's now early summer and the Easterly continues. The sea is choppy and I have to breathe on one side only. This section from Penzance to Marazion with its series of beach swims is the first time I've swum any distance over sand. Aside from the fun of the waves, the view under water is a bit boring and reminds me of the drudge of swimming lanes at the local pool. With precious little to see along this stretch, I fiddle with style, stroke and breathing. There's the occasional joy of a stone or fish and the odd jellyfish, but on the whole it's my namesake – sand, sand and more sand! So I lift my head to breathe more often than usual as the view up above is really glorious. Soft yellow beach and the Mount looming ever closer. It's just as well, as I'm lifting my head I spot a lone jet skier. He veers in too close and we pull up sharp. This guy is a potential hazard and his presence intrusive. Eventually he gets the message and jets off.

Waves ebb and flow over the large outflow pipe near our destination. I laugh out loud as we belly flop ourselves across the pipe like a pair of beached whales and sploosh back into the water to continue our struggle. It feels safe here in these waters – and at one point I realise I'm swimming along only a few feet from the bottom. This sand can be deceptive.

We spy the car park and chug towards it.

The fine sand turns to pebbles amongst which lie semi-precious stones such as lapis lazuli and malachite... apparently.

11. PADDLEBOARD SWIM

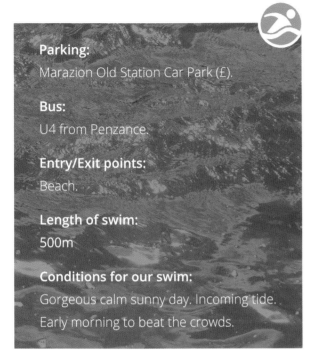

Parking:
Marazion Old Station Car Park (£).

Bus:
U4 from Penzance.

Entry/Exit points:
Beach.

Length of swim:
500m

Conditions for our swim:
Gorgeous calm sunny day. Incoming tide.
Early morning to beat the crowds.

Cake stop!

A reasonable selection in Marazion (see Little London Swim). We changed by the car and enjoyed the lovely morning with a coffee at Jordan's café - situated in a static kiosk on the car park. Don't let its outer shell fool you, this place serves simply great coffee and food (including cake and ice cream).

During the summer months there are 2 paddleboard stations at Marazion. The sun reflects on the sea sending a dazzle of silver in every direction. Within minutes we are tuned in to the gentle lapping of the water as it pushes us towards the Mount. This is high summer. There's a paddleboard lesson near the shore. Canoes head out to sea and children squeal in the shallows. Everyone is enjoying their ocean. We cross an area full of sea birds which is the natural outlet of a small freshwater stream that dashes through Ludgvan to the sea. It is called the Red River due to the deposits of iron hydroxide formed when water from old mine adits oozed into the rivers. The iron hydroxide lingers as a suspension and takes on an orange slimy hue which is unattractive but not poisonous. Nowadays it is clear and fresh – an area where birds gossip and preen. We pull up alongside the second paddleboard station and stroll back to the car park for coffee. Without doubt this is a leisurely swim and a great introduction to the Bay. Any newcomer to sea swimming will feel safe here and a sandy beach is definitely a good starting point for this project. Especially as the Mount provides such a spectacular backdrop. Swimming here today we feel the tensions of daily life evaporate.

9

LUGGERS
IN THE BAY

The lugger was the workforce of the Cornish fishing fleet for over 200 years. The fleet was huge with hundreds of boats setting out into the Bay to cast their nets in search of pilchards. But by 1918 they were virtually obsolete. During the 19th Century, pilchards were of particular value as not only was the fish itself extremely nutritious but once pressed the oil was used in lamps for lighting the streets of London and other cities. Now, the only Mount's Bay lugger remaining is the "Happy Return" which is owned by the Mount's Bay Association. However, other locally restored luggers also use the Bay and their rust red sails against a blue summer sky are a spectacular sight.

12. CAUSEWAY SWIM

Parking:
Marazion big Car Park (£)/St Michael's Mount Slipway Car Park (£).

Bus:
U4 from Penzance.

Entry/Exit points:
Beach.

Length of swim:
1000m

Conditions for our swim:
Stunning! Flat calm, blue skies and incoming tide.We went for an early morning swim to beat the crowds.

With perfect conditions this swim has everything. We are blown away by the variety of coastline that is contained in one kilometre.

Today we plan to round the spit of rock and swim into a hidden cove.

Our first objective is Chapel Rock, a small outcrop just off the beach which becomes an island when the tide is in. The rock represents the last shrine visited by pilgrims before going to the Mount. The chapel was destroyed in the 17th Century and we feel like aquatic pilgrims as we cross over the causeway and progress steadily to our destination. On the seaward side are hogus rocks formed when chunks of basaltic larva were explosively fragmented during a marine eruption.

The temperature soars and the Bay is flat and glassy. There's little tidal movement. A boat unloads its passengers and we keep an eye out for its return to the Mount. The sea bottom changes from sand to rock and seaweed.

We take in the sea walls of Marazion and head for a tiny beach as we round the point. We aim for a white painted tower but the water is so delightful that we swim on – past yet another spit (known as Top Tieb) and into the long sandy beach known as 'Little London'.

We clamber up the steps at the Western end of the beach and stroll back through the busy market town.

Cake stop!

We parked in the main Marazion car Park by the beach. Because the weather was so nice we went for an ice cream in the Beach Box situated in the car park. We had an average ice cream here and didn't try the coffee. See cafés in the Little London swim.

ST MICHAEL'S MOUNT

One stormy day in 495 AD St Michael, the archangel, descended onto a rock on the Western side of the Mount to guide a group of stranded fishermen to safety. The miracle transformed the island and it became a Christian stronghold for prayer and pilgrimage.

After the vision of St Michael , Celtic Christians established a monastery on the island. Pilgrims from Ireland and Wales crossed the causeway to pray and be granted absolution – for a fee. From the little harbour many pilgrims continued their journey, crossing into Europe to walk the path to Santiago de Compostela in Spain.

Alongside the Christian history is the legend of Jack the Giant slayer. The Mount was occupied by an evil giant known as Cormoran. Every year, this terrible ogre demanded human sacrifices from the mainland. One year a young man named Jack set out to destroy the giant and free the people of the mainland from their horrifying due. Young Jack dug a great hole covered it with brush and set his trap. When Cormoran strode into it he was snared and Jack killed him. He then tore out the giant's heart and threw it across the water to the mainland but it bounced back and is now buried in the steps to the Mount.

MARAZION TO PERRANUTHNOE

GEOLOGY AND ZOOLOGY

Bordering each end of Little London Bay are two spits known as Top Tieb and Little London rocks. The rock is a volcanic mix of granite and Mylor slate. These complex, crumpled patterns were formed by the energy of colliding continents. The contrast of hard and soft rock creates runnels and gullies providing an ideal habitat for marine wildlife. Here, rock pools harbour rare marine invertebrates and these flat intertidal reefs offer astonishing biodiversity.

Surprisingly, in this little known but beautiful Bay lives the best concentration of stalked jellyfish in the UK – Stauromedusae.

These little jellyfish are a bell-shaped animal with a stalk and a basal sucker. They have 8 tentacles and graze off algae moving around in cartwheels. They reproduce locally and it is thought that the storms of 2013-2014 may have been responsible for concentrating Stauromedusae in the more sheltered areas.

The shallow waters of this Bay are terrific for snorkelling and in the summer the seaweeds form an underwater garden.

13. LITTLE LONDON SWIM

Parking:
Marazion Car Parks (£)/on the street is free but time limited.

Bus:
U4 from Penzance.

Entry/Exit points:
Little London Beach off Leys Lane/Beach

Length of swim:
500m

Conditions for our swim:
Heavenly! Sun and gentle breeze. Incoming tide. Early morning.

The unspoilt bays of this stretch are difficult to access by car which is an advantage to swimmers as we can turn in at any point for a puff break and contemplate our ocean in solitude. The coves and bays are bordered by spits of rock which at high tide lengthen the distance of each swim but on a calm summer's day, when you and your partner manage to set up a rhythm, that perfect moment can be attained.

We head through the town and turn right down Leys Lane after the chapel, then left at a white gate and hey presto, we arrive on the most beautiful stretch of unspoilt beach.

Cake stop!

Marazion is a lovely place to spend some time – with little cafés and interesting shops and galleries. We chose coffee and fabulous cakes in the Copper Spoon café at the top of Leys Lane, but there's plenty of others including the Godolphin Hotel, 'The Horton Special' (water sports hire shop on the beach that has a little café too), the Chapel Rock Café (opposite the Godolphin) and, if you fancy popping over to the Mount (walk if the tide's out, boat or swim) there's the Sail Loft café by the harbour.

Once again there is not a cloud in the sky and the heat soars. As we swim towards Little London rocks at the Eastern end we browse like snorkelers amongst the rocks. Gentle currents swirl around us and we know it's time to get out and wait for another calm day to navigate the outcrop. It's too shallow to swim in across the rocks and too deep to clamber, so we back track a little to find a possible exit point. The steep sandstone cliffs are suffering erosion and a gatehouse with granite walls and steps overlooks this end of the Bay. This place could be a regular swim spot and we vow to return.

14. BASORE POINT

Parking:
Marazion or Perranuthnoe Car Park (£).

Bus:
U4 from Penzance (note the bus stops on the A30. 15 minute walk down the narrow road to Perranuthnoe Car Park)

Entry/Exit points:
Little London Beach/Basore Point

Length of swim: 1000m

Conditions for our swim:
A gentle Easterly with a light chop.

There is a problem of accessibility here so we are dropped off at the top of Leys Lane in Marazion and our watchers continue on to the Perranuthnoe Car Park. We walk the length of the beach to begin the next stage of our journey. High tide is early so we take the plunge at 7.30 in the morning just by Little London rocks. We aim to meet our watchers at our destination Basore Point, and for added impetus on the swim, they have our breakfast. This is the longest stretch of our journey, but on a such a beautiful day it was no chore.

The headland is not so little after all and it seems an age before Sand and I round the spit of Little London rock and swim on to yet another head of rock (Venton). A lone fisherman keeps an eye on us as we travel through but we're too far away to be hooked. The sun shines directly into our faces so it's difficult to get our bearings. We are conscious of swimming against the prevailing current as our buoys lag well behind. Perhaps that extra glass of wine the night before was a mistake. The rocks beneath keep me interested and I forget the distance. Reefs poke out into the sea and suddenly I can stand on a rock yet I'm 400m into the Atlantic. Rounding the second spit we enter Trenow Cove, another sweeping bay. We could end our swim here and take the coast path back to Marazion but once again, conditions are so good we plough on thinking of the picnic ahead.

Basore Point is at the far end of the bay, past yet another outcrop of rocks known as 'The Frenchman'. There's a granite bench marking the view point and I spot two pinheads. Are they our trusty watchers? Sound travels across the water and they hear our staccato bursts of conversation.

"My hat won't stay on," yells Sand, shattering the peace.

"Pull it over yer ears."

Seagulls flutter off the water.

"It's too dark. My goggles are too dark." I grumble.

"That's only the sun in your eyes. It's the same for me."

Cormorants turn and hang out their wings to dry. Wading birds whistle and swoop above us. We spot godwits – they have the long straight beak and not the curved one. Bar-tailed or black tailed I cannot tell. Now we begin to slog it out. Although a busy mining area in the past, Trenow Cove is a wonderful secluded spot.

Our watchers are waving and we've almost made it. We slip and slide amongst the rocks and it's a bothersome exit. Our watchers haul us out, pat us on the back and we all stroll back to Perranuthnoe beach.

Cake stop!
We brought our own for this one – see next swim for Perranuthnoe.

15. PERRANUTHNOE SWIM

Parking:
Perranuthnoe Car Park (£).

Bus:
U4 from Penzance (bus drop off on A30, 15 min walk to Perranuthnoe Car Park).

Entry/Exit points:
Basore Point beach/Perranuthnoe beach.

Length of swim:
1000m

Conditions for our swim:
Another gorgeous day with a light Westerly. Incoming springtide. Another early morning start.

It's an easy walk in our wetsuits and with our watchers and our trusty dog Poppy, we trek out past the tamarisk trees to the little wooden ladder that takes us down onto the shingly beach. This is definitely a good spot for smuggling booty. We can see it all from the sea. This cove is known as Trevelyan Cove or Blight Harvey's Cove –

we wonder for a moment just what Trevelyan or Harvey did to get a cove named after them, maybe we'll find treasure on the way?

Today the wind is with us. Although the sea surges a little around the rocks it's not a problem. To our right is a separate island, The Greeb. At certain times of the year it is possible to walk there – with your back pack on your head and a waterproof pair of shorts. The island seems a way out on this spring tide but it provides a safe haven for many unusual birds although not the grebe!

We swim on, marvelling at the sights both above and below the water. Although we appear to be a way off shore, the intricate rocky outcrops form wonderful

pools and caverns. One moment we're swimming almost within touching distance of the rocks – the next we see nothing but blackness below.

We past 'The Bears' rocks and finally reach Maen du Point, the last headland, very quickly and as we round the point we spy our final destination.

Perran Sands, at Perranuthnoe, approaches very quickly and we head towards the slip, coasting in with the waves. The sand shines like gold in the morning sun – perhaps we have found the treasure after all?

All too soon it seems, we have reached our final destination – for the time being anyway!

Cake stop!

There are a few little cafés and a good pub (The Victoria) in Perranuthnoe. We tended to bring picnics each time we came here as we had early morning swims and the nearest café to the beach (The Cabin) wasn't yet open.

WILD SWIMMING IN CORNWALL

The largest site with the most information about swimming in the West Country is the Devon and Cornwall Wild Swimming site (www.devonandcornwallwildswimming.co.uk) which is packed with information, reading material and tips.

The Cornwall Wild Swimmers have a Facebook page with more local information readily available. But to narrow open-water swimming down to the Penzance area then look no further than the group called 'The Battery Belles and Buoys'. The founder member is Tina Riggall who kindly wrote our foreword. If you are seeking a social swim then this group of cheerful folk swim off Battery Rocks every morning.

The Cornwall Wild Swimmers will occasionally post details of an impromptu swim around the Mount (a distance of around 2.2 km) which usually has canoe support. We were lucky enough to participate in one of these swims on a calm July evening. Our canoeist stuck by us and took some excellent photos.

TWO BONUS SWIMS

'CAUSEWAY DEPENDENCY' SWIM

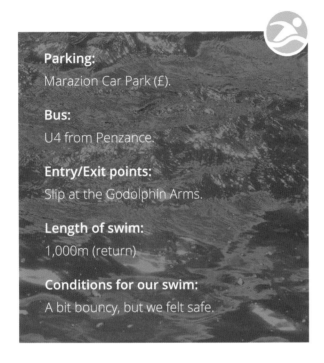

Parking:
Marazion Car Park (£).

Bus:
U4 from Penzance.

Entry/Exit points:
Slip at the Godolphin Arms.

Length of swim:
1,000m (return)

Conditions for our swim:
A bit bouncy, but we felt safe.

We stand at the bottom of a stepped slip on a humid overcast day. The sea sluices up and over the steps in a churning and unfriendly manner.

"We'll keep Chapel Rock to our right and seek out the causeway immediately. Then all we have to do is follow it." I say optimistically.

"Keep an eye out for the gigs which are launching now, and that canoe, and don't forget the sailing club has a race shortly." You're right Sand – there's always a lot going on in this channel.

We fix our buoys firmly around our waists and stride into the water. It's a sandy start – we can touch the bottom and although visibility isn't great we dodge the floating islands of seaweed and head out towards Chapel Rock. The coral coloured squares of the smooth granite causeway soon appear and we turn to follow the cobblestone road. We look up every 15 strokes or so. The ferry is still taking visitors off the island but the boatman can see us and steers away. We bob wildly in the wake but the waves don't settle. It's a little more bouncy out here than we anticipated. Below us the causeway acts as a perfect guide.

The water is deeper here and for a few minutes I lose the causeway. I've allowed myself to be dependent on a variable. So I take cues from the land ahead. I can see the slip and imagine the course of the yellow brick road beneath me. It soon reappears, Sand is following close behind and the sea becomes calmer as we head towards the outer wall of the harbour.

It's a good feeling to be the only people on the island. We patter round into the harbour and enjoy a few minutes alone. Perhaps Lord St Levan is looking down at us from his castle wondering

whether we are about to film an advert for Cadbury's Milk Tray. But the intrepid explorers do not leap from the pier all dressed in black nor do they linger. It's quite chilly in the early autumn gloom and they have to return. This time we swim with the tide and the journey is faster. A canoeist is gently tracking our course and I veer towards Sand who swims, as usual, in a perfect straight line.

Now we swim side by side in synchrony. Arms rise. Faces turn to breathe. Our stroke is matched and although we don't speak, spirits soar and we enter that peculiar swimming state of quiet elation which is difficult to beat on land. All too soon we're being sluiced up the steps by the tide. I'm cold but very, very satisfied with life.

ST CLEMENT'S ISLE

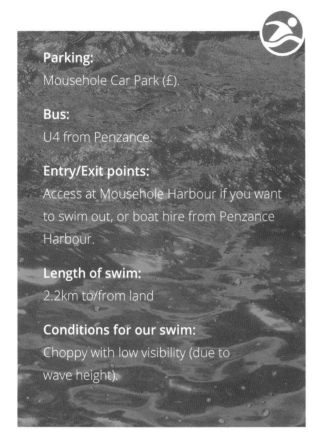

Parking:
Mousehole Car Park (£).

Bus:
U4 from Penzance.

Entry/Exit points:
Access at Mousehole Harbour if you want to swim out, or boat hire from Penzance Harbour.

Length of swim:
2.2km to/from land

Conditions for our swim:
Choppy with low visibility (due to wave height).

The channel from the harbour to the island is often busy with boating traffic but as long as the swimmer wears the brightly coloured buoy then they are safe enough.

I receive a call from Sand whose home overlooks the Bay.

"It's flat calm here," she says in her usual chirpy fashion. Well, it would be flat calm – that's why your patch of sea is called Gwavas Lake – emphasis on the Lake. Up here in Sancreed, the wind is blowing hard and we are suffering a heavy bout of Cornish mist.

"I'll muster boat support." I mutter into the phone feeling edgy.

We have swum this island before and I know why it is a favourite for swimmers. The sense of adventure and achievement guarantees a high.

Sand and I are togged up and wait on the pontoon in Penzance Harbour for the boat. Simon picks us up and steers us gently out into open water. We are travelling against both the wind and the swell. Our little boat leaps the peaks and crashes into the troughs. Everyone aboard studies the grey ocean with pursed lips. Even 'flat-calm' Sand is a little fazed. Simon slows the boat on the approach to the island. Sure enough there's a group of seals and a posse of cormorants looking like ragged schoolboys in detention. The animal life observes us with a critical eye.

For extra safety we have brought an escort – not agency hired to entertain, but a strong swimmer who will accompany us round. The boat will follow us so we've taken every precaution.

We choose to swim harbour-side against the swell and round the back of the island for the speedy last leg. Sand, myself and Rupert plunge from the boat. The water is unexpectedly cold. High tide is about 40 minutes away and as we begin our anti-clockwise swim, I am aware of the strength of the swell and current. I don't seem to be making any progress at all. It is impossible to see my fellow swimmers through the chop but the boat is there, steadily tracking our progress. White water crashes against the Westerly side of the island and that iron mount forming the frame for a fantastic Christmas light display just never retreats from my vision. The seals accompany us, as does a day boat which is, in turn, tracking the seals. Several compass jellyfish glide by. I am past caring. Stopping for a puff break is counter-productive. I have to hurl my body out of the water to see anything at all. Keep going, I silently chant. Keep going. And suddenly we're round the bend – in more ways than one!

The swell is pretty big but we are with it which feels fantastic. Everyone is swimming at a terrific pace. However, my eyes are not on the island, the seals or the bird life. I want that boat. But it is moving with the currents faster than I can swim.

"Wait – we've finished. Wait for us."

It's another ungainly exit from the water and I flop around on the floor of the boat like a hooked mackerel. 20 minutes of hard work against the swell and 5 minutes with it. That was St Clement's Isle. I think I'll re-name it St Element's Isle. It's all there in one short, arduous swim.

Cake stop!

After such a challenging swim we felt we deserved a treat, so headed to the rather lovely Old Coastguard Hotel which overlooks St Clement's Isle.

On a warm day the beautiful garden is an ideal recovery spot – and you can re-live the swim all over again. Feeling somewhat chilly we went indoors and sank into the plush armchairs to enjoy an excellent coffee and a big slice of cake.

14

ST CLEMENT'S ISLE

Strangely enough the island is not named after Clemo's, the extraordinary hardware shop in St Just but after Clemens, a Christian king of part of Cornwall in around 600 AD. When his son Petroc refused the kingship to devote his life to Christianity and travel to Jerusalem, Clemens retired to this little island and became a hermit. It is believed the island had a chapel and on that site spears and axes of copper have been found wrapped in linen. Today it is inhabited only by birds and seals. St Clement's Isle is a favourite wild swimming destination but a quick reccy before swimming around the island is highly recommended.

A MEETING OF MINDS

Penny and Sand met through art. Having seen Penny's paintings on display in Penzance, Sand tracked down the artist to her rural retreat.

Penny: *She didn't just drop in. She burst in. Then she clacked across the studio in her heels, peered over my shoulder at the offering on the easel and in her sing-song Liverpudlian accent said, 'I loove it!'*

Sand: *It was the way she captured the sea. There was so much energy. It didn't take me long to choose a couple of paintings.*

Penny: *So, I drove over to Newlyn to deliver and hang the art but was distracted by the amazing view of Mount's Bay from Sand's house.*

Sand: *That was when Penny told me she'd just finished a freestyle swimming course in the local pool and was practising in the Bay. This was such a coincidence as I'd just learned everything I know about front crawl from 'You Tube' and I was also trying it out in the sea!*

Outside, the sea was placid. Silver light bounced off the water sending a signal to the two ladies above. The hanging could wait. It was time to practise their new skill for real...

ACKNOWLEDGEMENTS

We would like to thank Tina for her help, advice and for writing the foreword. Also, a big thank you to Rupert who accompanied us on the more hair-raising swims. And thank you Darren from Treganna Design (www.tregannadesign.co.uk) for helping us lay out this book.

Thank you Jeff Goodman and Mark Milburn for supplying the underwater photos of the 3 jellyfish and a seal.

And finally thank you to our watchers, Al, Simon and Poppy the dog who kept their eye on us on the longer swims, gave us boat support and made sure that the picnics were neatly laid out when we finally staggered from the ocean blue.

LIST OF PAINTINGS

For more information regarding the
paintings please contact Penny Rumble
penny@pennyrumble.com
www.pennyrumble.com